Emma S. Clark Memorial Library Setauket

Orient Pt. Light

The Ancient House of Cutchogue

Whaling Museum Sag Harbor

Benj. Thompson Historian

Old Thompson House Setauket

Stony Brook Post Office

Suffolk Museum Stony Brook

Orient Point

Plum Island

Orient

Greenport

Shelter Island

Gardiner's Island

Montauk Point

Southold

Peconic

Montauk

Cutchogue

Grass Hollow

Kings town

Powder Hill

Freetown

Devon

Napeague Beach

Old Hook Mill East Ham.

Mattituck

Sag Harbor

Amagansett

Pontigo

North ville

Roanoke

Franklinville

Laurie

Great Peconic Bay

Noyack

East Hampton

James-port

Deerfield

Scuttlehole

Bridge-hampton

John Howard Payne

Wading River

Baiting Hollow

Aquebogue

Riverhead

North Sea

Water Mill

Hayground

Medox

Payne's Home East Hampton

Sag Harbor

Calverton

Hampton Park

Tuckahoe

Cobb

Shinnecock Hills

Halsey Homestead Southampton 1648

Ridge

Flanders

Hampton Bays

Southampton

Manorville

Oakville

Spring-ville

South Manor

Eastport

Westhampton

Quiogue Quogue

Speonk

Quiodue

South Moriches Center

East Moriches

Remsenburg

South Haven

Moriches

Shinnecock Indians

Westhampton Beach

Mastic Beach

Smith's Pt.

The Big Duck of Flanders

Gateway Playhouse Bellport

The Manor St. George

Smith's Point

Passing Montauk Light

Long Island

Done by
Catherine & E. Theodo
St. James, N. Y.

© 1964

D1088054

OUR LONG ISLAND

OUR LONG ISLAND

Second Edition

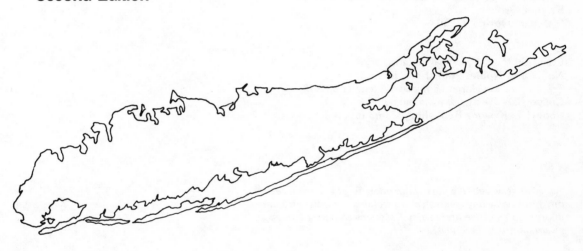

George Mannello

Robert E. Krieger Publishing Company, Inc.
Malabar, Florida
1981

Original Edition 1964
Second Edition 1981

Printed and Published by
ROBERT E. KRIEGER PUBLISHING CO., INC.
Krieger Drive
Malabar, Florida 32950

Library of Congress Cataloging in Publication Data

Mannello, George, 1913-
  Our Long Island.

  1. Long Island. I. Title.
F127.L8M26 1981   974.7'21   80-21211
ISBN 0-88275-968-X

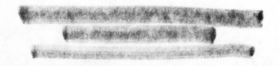

Preface

This revival of *Our Long Island* under a new publisher incorporates changes that both update and improve the text. The book, as before, has been written at a seventh grade level. Its renaissance coincides with a recent renewed interest, sparked by *Newsday*, in the study of the Long Island community. Moreover, during a personal conference with high ranking officials of the State Department of Education Bureau of Social Studies in Albany during February, 1979, I was assured that, despite considerable revision of the social studies curriculum some years ago, local studies has remained a highly desired part of the seventh grade program.

It seems we repeat history. Today, as in 1950 prior to the publication of the earlier volume, I find to my dismay few adequate materials available for students. Long Island, especially that part outside of New York City, deserves its own textbook. After all, it has more people than most of our states do.

George Mannello

Contents

LONG ISLAND

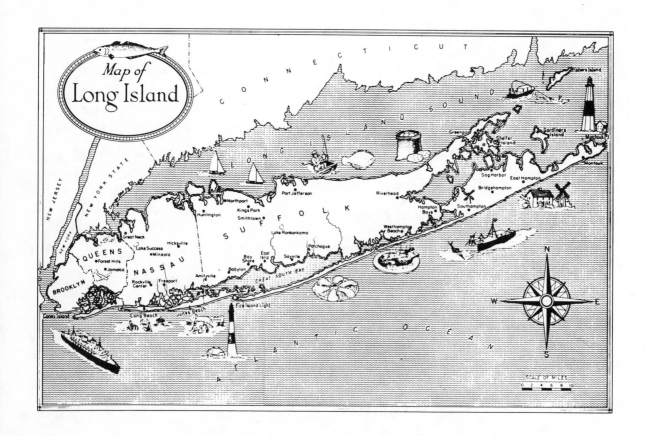

THE MAP OF LONG ISLAND RESEMBLES A BIG FISH

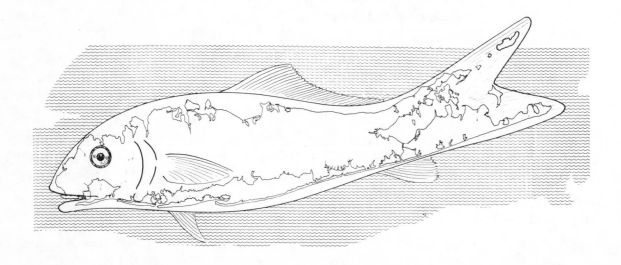

CHAPTER 1

Geography of Long Island

If you have a good imagination and a map of New York State, it is not difficult to see that Long Island is really a great big fish. The fish's head snuggles close to the shore where New York City is, nibbling on a fat, juicy worm which we call Manhattan. His tail floats lazily to the east in the Atlantic Ocean.

It was thus that many of the early inhabitants of Long Island viewed the land. As a matter of fact, in keeping with the fish story, the ridges that run along the north side of the island have been called the "backbone" and the two peninsulas which thrust into the Atlantic Ocean on the east end have been known as "flukes," one the North Fluke and the other the South Fluke. The work *fluke*, as used by fishermen, means one of the fins of the tail of a whale.

It is easy to understand why Long Island has been compared to a fish. Fishing, you will find, has been and continues to be, an important industry on our island. In the early days, Long Island was claimed by Connecticut. New York State landed a very good catch when it hooked Long Island. Perhaps it was because of the fine bait used—Manhattan Isle. Long Island could never resist the rich trade which New York City offered, and today, as well as in early times, one of the chief reasons for the prosperity found on Long Island is New York City.

SOME NUMBER FACTS

Long Island measures about 118 miles in length from New York Bay to Montauk Point. It is approximately twenty miles at its widest point, from Lloyds Neck to Seaford, but its average width is about fifteen miles. It is the largest island belonging to the United States directly off the mainland coast. Its total area is 1,723 square miles, which makes Long Island larger than the state of Rhode Island. Long Island is the only part of New York State which has an ocean frontage.

Long Island's importance is far out of proportion to its size. In 1980, 6,900,000 people lived on the island, a population exceeded by only a few states. This is two fifths of the population of New York State.

Let us get clear what is meant by Long Island. We can think of Long Island in the geographic sense. This includes all the land that was described above. Also, we can think of Long Island in the popular sense—how people usually regard it. This is different and it includes only two of the four Long Island counties. In this case only the counties of Suffolk and Nassau are Long Island. The other two counties, Queens and Kings (Brooklyn) are part of New York City.

In addition, there are a few large islands off the coast which are incorporated with Suffolk County. These include Fishers Island, Gardiners Island, Plum Island and Shelter Island, all located in the eastern waters of Long Island. By counties the population in 1976 was: Kings 2,398,000; Queens 1,968,000; Nassau, 1,468,000; and Suffolk 1,316,000.

CLIMATE

Long Island has a comparatively good climate. Jutting into the Atlantic Ocean as it does, being surrounded on all sides by water, its climate is seldom extreme. The ocean which flows past Long Island's south shore has a tempering effect on the weather. That is, it helps make Long Island cool in the summer and mild in the winter. This happens because the breeze blowing from the sea in July and August is cooled by the colder water. Then the breeze cools the land over which it blows. In the winter the water is warmer than the land and, hence, the wind coming from the sea warms the land.

The temperature seldom goes below 10 degrees in the winter, nor above 90 degrees during the summer. Throughout the year average temperatures are comfortable, about 60 degrees during the day and 39 degrees during the night. Your school room is normally kept at a temperature of 68 to 70 degrees because this is considered a good climate for human beings while sitting indoors.

The weather on Long Island is warm enough and sunny enough so that the farmers have a growing season lasting 200 days of the year.

Long Island is fortunate in having sunshine on the average of 70 percent of the days of a month. On the other hand, we have enough rain to guarantee Long Island's position as a leading agricultural district of the state. The average rainfall is 43 inches a year. This is spread over twelve months so that, normally, too much rain does not fall in any one month, a very important fact for farmers.

THE SOUTH SHORE

To get to know what it looks like let us take an imaginary automobile trip around Long Island. As we travel find the places that we visit on the map on page 3. We start from Manhattan and go through the Brooklyn-Battery Tunnel that connects Manhattan with Long Island. Coming out of the tunnel we can see a large body of water on the right hand side. This is New York Bay, one of the most important harbors in the world. We take the Belt Parkway to the South Shore of the Island, bypassing the heavy traffic in Kings County.

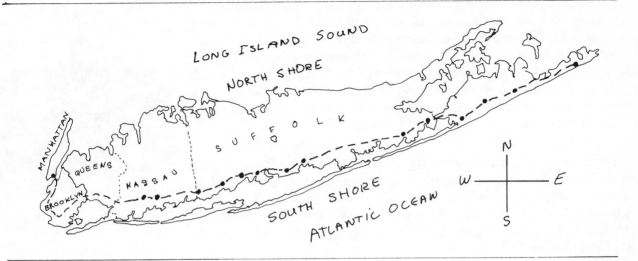

While Kings (Brooklyn) is the smallest of the Long Island counties in size, for wealth and population it is the most important. Later we shall spend some time there when we discuss the history and the economic development of Long Island.

One thing we must understand before proceeding any further is what is meant by North, South, East and West on Long Island. Long Island directions are sometimes confusing when compared to the rest of the country along the eastern seaboard of the United States. Much of the traffic along the Atlantic Coast runs north and south. In our own state we speak of "upstate," meaning the northern part. For the most part traffic on Long Island runs east and west, into and out of New York City. When we speak of the South Shore, we mean that coast of Long Island which is along the Atlantic Ocean. The North Shore fronts Long Island Sound.

Proceeding with our trip, then we take the South Shore highways going toward Montauk Point, the most easterly part of the island. If we were in a hurry to get to Montauk, we would take one of the fine parkways that extend eastward from New York City through the lovely, parkway strips bypassing the villages along the way. But we are in no hurry, so let us take the old Merrick Road.

As we roll through the suburban villages, through Valley Stream, Lynbrook, Rockville Centre, Baldwin, and Freeport, we see how flat the land is. If we take a side road down to the water to the less settled areas we will notice that the soil is very sandy, full of sea shells. In fact, there are so many sea shells on Long Island that the Dutch settlers called it Seawanhakie, meaning "Island of Shells." Sometimes on digging down into the soil, one may strike a whole layer of old sea shells. Tough grasses help keep the sand down, but even so, the salty wind coming from the ocean whips it into our faces.

This South Shore plain extends the whole length of Long Island, varying in width from one to eleven miles. It starts from the hilly North Shore and gradually slopes toward the south, dropping at the rate of abouut twenty feet in every mile, until it meets the sea. Around Hempstead it is called the Hempstead Plains. The Hempstead Plains is good land for farming and in the old days this central part of Long Island running far into Suffolk County was one of the most important agricultural districts of the state. Today it is built up with one family houses, shopping centers and factories.

The eastern part of this plain is made up of what is called the Pine Barrens. These are large sand and clay areas which are not very fertile. Efforts to grow crops here have met with failure. Short pine trees grow along with other stunted trees such as the bayberry, from which candles were once made, the beach plum and the dwarfed red cedar. Years ago forest fires laid waste to much of this territory.

(Courtesy of Nassau County Historical M

HEMPSTEAD PLAINS

FRESH WATER ON LONG ISLAND

Perhaps you have noticed in our travels so far that Long Island has practically no internal waterways, that is, rivers and lakes. You will find a few short streams along the South Shore, flowing lazily toward the ocean, and you will find a small lake or two, but nothing like the magnificent waterways of upstate New York. The largest lake on Long Island is Lake Ronkonkoma which measures about three miles in circumference. It has a depth of 83 feet. Lake Ronkonkoma is peculiar in that it has no inlet nor outlet. This is because it is fed and drained by underground springs which are found in many parts of the island.

Most drinking water on Long Island comes from underground springs. Some of the underground water comes from the mainland across Long Island Sound. Or, rain water soaks into the ground and slowly flows in regular streams toward the ocean. Wells are sunk into the soil and the water is pumped into small reservoirs or into tanks.

EASTERN LONG ISLAND

On we go, eastward through Babylon, Bayshore, and Patchogue along the Great South Bay, and through the Moriches. We go through the Shinnecock Hills, the Hamptons and finally out on the peninsula ending with Montauk Point. This is the South Fork of Long Island. The North Fork ends at Orient Point.

It is on this eastern end of Long Island that we notice some of the land's most interesting features. The sea is all around you, wherever you look. A strong wind blows continually, creating a salty, sticky feeling. The early colonists built windmills in this region, a few of which are still standing today, to put the wind to work grinding their wheat and corn. Today, people once more are thinking

of building windmills—modern, more efficient ones to make electricity. Notice how the wind blows the sand into little hills. Tomorrow these hills will be blown away and others will take their place somewhere else. These sand hills, found along the whole South Shore, are called sand dunes. They never stay in one place, so the shore line of Long Island is never the same; it is always changing.

LIGHTHOUSE AT MONTAUK POINT
Note how the ocean waves have eaten away the shore line. Here at the extreme eastern end of Long Island, fishing is a popular sport.

Notice, also, how the waves beat against the shore. Like the wind, these waves are changing the Long Island shore line. When the Montauk Lighthouse was first built in 1795, it stood 297 feet from the edge of the bluff upon which it is situated. Today, because of the action of the waves, it is only about one hundred feet from the edge. The waves have pushed the land back, and the current of the ocean flowing from Montauk Point toward the west, has strung the sand out into long thin beaches. Look at your map and you will see the narrow, long "barrier beaches," as they are called. They are walls of sand pushed up by the ocean waves. They form a barrier between the main part of Long Island and the Atlantic Ocean.

HIGHWAY NEAR MONTAUK POINT
Note the low, level countryside and the sand dunes with the Atlantic Ocean in the background.

These barrier beaches are probably familiar to you. They include Fire Island, Oak Island, Jones Beach, Long Beach, Far Rockaway and Coney Island. When Rockaway Peninsula was surveyed in 1925 it was found to be four miles longer than it was when first surveyed in 1835. Thus, the ocean current has gradually eaten away the eastern part of Long Island and has built up the western end. During the 1938 hurricane and 1962 storm the ocean overflowed the barrier beaches into the bays beyond, destroying millions of dollars' worth of buildings which had been erected upon this land.

In between the beaches and the mainland of Long Island, broad shallow bays were created in which are found the famous Long Island oysters and clams. These waterways include Jamaica Bay, Great South Bay, Moriches Bay and Shinnecock Bay. This is where the marsh meadows are. The land is covered with marsh grass, but is too spongy and soggy to be of much use to man.

Coming back along the South Fork from Montauk Point, we go through Sag Harbor which, a hundred twenty five years ago, was the center of a prosperous whaling industry. It lies in the tail of the great Long Island fish between Peconic Bay and Gardiners Bay, well protected from the pounding ocean waves.

Northward across the water lies Shelter Island. To the east lies romantic Gardiners Island, scene of adventures of the famous pirate, Captain Kidd. Gardiners Island is privately held land today, having been owned by the Gardiner family ever since 1639. Fishers Island, which is near the coast of Connecticut, belongs to Long Island only in name. Its inhabitants do business with Connecticut and not with New York. It was originally named Vischer after a Dutch explorer.

(Courtesy of Nicholas Basilion

BEACH SCENE

THE NORTH SHORE

We travel through Riverhead, county seat of Suffolk County, and then back along the North Shore toward New York City. We pass through Rocky Point, Port Jefferson, Northport and Huntington, curving around the numerous coves and onto the many "necks" that extend into Long Island Sound. Long Island Sound is the large body of water along the North Shore that separates Long Island from the mainland.

As we travel westward, we notice that the country is becoming more hilly, more rocky. The coast line is more irregular than it is on the South Shore. Here is wooded and pasture land watered by many brooks. We are constantly surprised after topping a hill to come down abruptly into a cozy little cove like Cold Spring Harbor. The Sound comes in and nestles in the charming bays. Trees overhang deep water. The North Shore is a pleasant contrast after the sandy flatlands of southern Long Island.

The "necks" are especially interesting pieces of land. They really are peninsulas stretching into the Sound. A peninsula is a land formation surrounded on three sides by water.

Long Island, as you must have discovered by now, is bristling with peninsulas. There are Rockaway Peninsula, the North Fork, the South For, Eaton's Neck, Lloyd's Neck and Great Neck, to mention only a few of the larger ones. As on the South Shore, the peninsulas or necks along the North Shore were created by the waves.

In contrast to what is found along the South Shore, high bluffs are common on the North Shore of the island. They rise sharply out of the water, sometimes to a height of two hundred feet. These bluffs are made of soft clay and sand. The action of the waves dashing unceasingly against their sides causes them to cave in. During a long period, this action has carved out many of the little inlets found along the North Shore. It has also helped join little islands off the coast to the mainland of Long Island. By caving in the sides of the high bluffs on the islands and on the mainland, a connecting neck of land has been formed. Thus a peninsula is born.

(Courtesy of Nassau County Historical Museum)

DUNES AND OCEAN

LONG ISLAND SOIL

Along the North Shore occasionally we pass by deep man-made sand pits. These pits are examples of the only real mining that is practiced on Long Island. Also, they tell us what lies underneath the surface of the land.

And what do we see? Why, nothing but sand and gravel. Sometimes there is some clay. This is an interesting fact about Long Island soil: except for the western edges of Brooklyn and Queens, there is no large mass of rocks near the surface. Wells have been dug down 1100 feet without finding any bedrock.

The sand on Long Island varies from fine and white to coarse and yellow, depending upon how far one digs down or from what section of the Island it is taken. The gravel is smooth and round. The clay may be white, brown, blue or yello. On most of Long Island the top soil which covers these minerals is not very deep. Because of this, the roots of large trees must grown horizontally instead of growing straight down into the sand. It also means that the Long Island farmer must spend much money on fertilizer to keep what little soil he has producing crops.

From Huntington we head inland for the Northern State Parkway, one of the beautiful park roads which the state built on Long Island. We are on the last leg of our journey. The road runs along the top of a ridge; the terrain is strewn with small rocks here, as it is all along the North Shore. This is one of the highest parts of Long Island, though Long Island is not very high any place. The highest spot is High Hill (Jayne's Hill) near Walt Whitman's birthplace, which rises to a height of 410 feet. The Empire State Building in New York City is three times the height of High Hill.

SAND PIT AT SMITHTOWN

NORTHERN STATE PARKWAY

As we enter the Borough of Queens along this Parkway, we catch a glimpse of the suburbs of New York City. Extending toward the south, level land can be seen skirting the ridge upon which we are traveling. For miles and miles there are little suburban homes crowding on top of each other much like rows of army tents. While we are riding in the hills, what is seen down below seems amazingly flat.

LONG ISLAND'S GLACIERS

The story of the land formation of this part of Long Island is the most interesting of all. As we mentioned earlier, the ridge which runs east and west along the northern side of Long Island has been called its backbone. Long ago, during the Ice Age, much of North America was covered by a glacier. A glacier is a huge sheet of ice which may be hundreds of feet tall. It is made as one snowfall after another packs so tightly that the heavy snow seems to be ice. It forms only when the weather is cold enough so that the snows does not melt. It keeps piling up, getting harder and harder. When the pile is large enough there is tremendous pressure from its weight, and the glacier begins to spread out. Nothing can stand in its way when it moves. The only thing which stops a glacier is a change in the weather which will make it melt.

The ice sheet which covered North America crept down out of the cold North, destroying everything before it. Animals ran away toward the South, and vegetation died. Four such ice sheets visited Long Island. The last one, the Wisconsin Ice Sheet, came in two layers. The ice was hundreds of feet high. As it inched forward, it picked up many loose things such as rocks, earth and boulders and carried them with it.

The glacier met the ocean where Long Island stands today and went no farther. Then, about 40,000 years ago, it began to melt and draw back. But in doing so, it left all the loose materials, which it had been carrying, at that spot where the ice melted. That is why there are high rocky hills on the northern side of Long Island. These are called terminal moraines. A terminal moraine is a hill left behind at the end of an ice sheet. The two layers of the Wisconsin Ice Sheet left the South Fork and the North Fork. In fact, it left two easily seen ridges across all of northern Long Island. The glacier also left certain hollowed out pieces of land which are known as kettles. Lake Ronkonkoma and Lake Success are two kettle lakes.

As the ice melted, the water flowed down the ridges toward the ocean carrying with it the soft part of the hills. This formed the plains to the south. In addition, as the ages went by, the action of the rain, wind, heat and cold upon the rocks broke them up to form the fertile Hempstead Plains. Such plains are known as alluvial plains and are excellent for farming.

However, there are still many rocks left on the North Shore. If you have ever been to bathe at any of the North Shore swimming beaches, you know that it is a rocky area. An extra large rock is the glacial boulder, measuring fifty-four by forty feet, found southwest of Manhasset.

Northern Long Island is a geologist's idea of heaven. A geologist is a person who studies what the earth is made of. Here, the geologist can find in a few miles a great variety of different stones. These stones date from all ages. Some go back only 50,000 years, while the oldest go back over 2 billion years. It would take a geologist a long time traveling over a great area, to collect in some other part of the country the stones which he can quickly pick up on Long Island. They include trap rock, garnet, red sandstone, white quartz, black slate, mica, feldspar, granite and limestone. The ice sheet very conveniently lifted these rocks from different places as it traveled and deposited them in one big heap on Long Island.

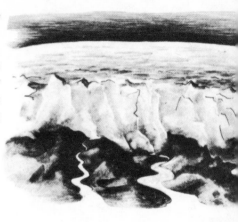

ICE GLACIERS ONCE COVERED LONG ISLA

There is just one more thing to remember as we roll into New York City on the Queensboro Bridge. That body of water down below, known as the East River, is not a river at all. It is a strait or channel through which the ocean tide flows, connecting Long Island Sound with New York Bay—thus making Long Island really an island.

QUEENSBORO BRIDGE LOOKING EAST FROM MANHATTAN TOWARD LONG ISLAND CITY
Since this bridge was built, there have been several other bridges and tunnels constructed to carry the heavy automobile and truck traffic between Long Island and New York City.

SUMMARY

Two powerful natural forces have taken a hand in shaping Long Island. The great glaciers have deposited much of the soil upon which we now live. Then the ocean currents have changed the shore line, wearing away the sides and building up peninsulas. Long Island is a flat but highly important piece of land. Its climate and its location near New York City make our island a desirable place for millions of people to live.

WHAT WORDS ARE MISSING?

Long Island is shaped like a (1). It measures (2) miles in length and averages (3) miles in width. Its area is (4) square miles. The population for my county is (5). Long Island's climate is tempered by the (6). Its average daytime temperature throughout the year is (7). The level part in the center of the Island is known as the (8). The shape of the land on the South Shore is (9) while the North Shore is (10). The largest lake on Long Island is named (11). Most drinking water on Long Island comes from (12). The long strips of land off the southern coast of Long Island are called (13). The shore line of Long Island is constantly being changed by the (14). Three minerals found on Long Island are (15, 16, and 17). The ridges running down the middle of the Island were brought by (18). They are scientifically known as (19).

CHAPTER THINKING

The ocean plays an important part in shaping the geography of Long Island. Explain what this means.

Long Island is a geologist's paradise. What does this mean and why is it so?

Give some reasons why Long Island has such a large population.

ACTIVITIES

1. Draw an outline map of Long Island and show the following land features. Add any others that you know.

North Fork	Rockaway Peninsula
South Fork	Fire Island
Montauk Point	Lloyds Neck
Gardiners Island	Shinnecock Hills
Fishers Island	Hempstead Plains
Shelter Island	Barrier beaches
Orient Point	North Shore bluffs

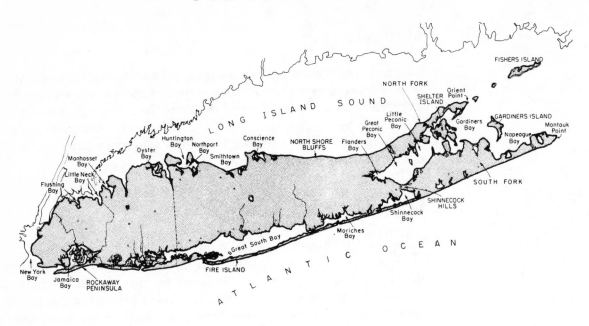

2. Draw an outline map showing the following waterways. Add any others that you know.

New York Bay   Gardiners Bay
Jamaica Bay   Lake Ronkonkoma
Great South Bay   East River
Moriches Bay   Oyster Bay
Shinnecock Bay   Cold Spring Harbor
Peconic Bay   Long Island Sound

3. Construct a salt and flour map of Long Island.

4. Make a collection of different kinds of minerals found on Long Island.

5. Plan an automobile trip around Long Island. On an automobile map trace the route you will take and the villages you will pass through. Plan your trip so that you see many of the geographic features mentioned in this chapter.

6. On a map, mark a boat trip in a small cabin cruiser around Long Island, using as many bays and protected waters along the South Shore as you can. At what places would you dock your boat?

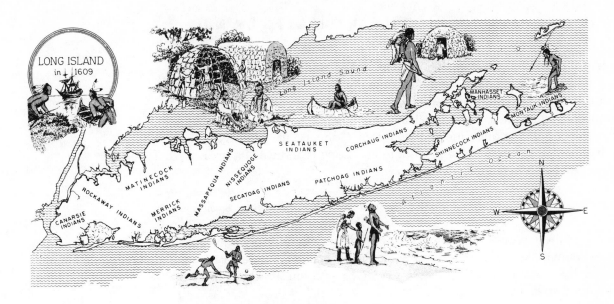

LOCATION OF INDIAN TRIBES ON LONG ISLAND

CHAPTER 2

The Indians of Paumanok

When the first settler came to Long Island in the middle of 1600's, he found here a number of Indians who welcomed him into their midst and befriended him. In contrast with the more warlike tribes of the Iroquois in upper New York State and the Narragansetts of New England across the Sound, Long Island Indians were peaceloving and settled. Indeed, they even paid tribute in the form of wampum to larger and more powerful tribes on the mainland. In other words they made forced payments of precious shell beads called wampum. So, when Europeans came to settle on Long Island, they did not have to face the danger of an Indian uprising which was common in some of the other colonies.

THE THIRTEEN TRIBES

When Hempstead was first settled in 1643, there were about 6500 Indians on Long Island. They lived in groups which we call tribes. These tribes were much too small to compare with, or compete against, the tribes of the mainland. They were actually large families with almost everyone related to everyone else with the group. Because of their way of life as hunters and fishers the Indians did not live together in large groups. Therefore, when a tribe became too large, a group broke away from the main body, elected a new chief and became independent. There were thirteen of these Long Island Indian "tribes" in 1643.

Long Island Indians came from Algonquian stock, the Indian race which inhabited the eastern seaboard of what is now the United States. Those who lived in the western half of the Island belonged to the Delaware family of the Algonquians, while those who inhabited the eastern half were related to another Algonquian group, the Mohegans of Connecticut. However, the name that was used in reference to all of Indian Long Island was Paumanok, meaning "land of tribute."

Incidentally, you must not be confused if you happen to see several spellings for the same Indian name. Even to this day we cannot quite decide how to spell some of these names. For instance, the word Paumanok appears in some books as Paumanake and in others as Paumanack. Setauket and Seatalcot are names for the same Indian tribe. It seems our early colonists were not particularly good spellers!

The Long Island Indian tribe, then, was simply a number of families living together under a head man known as a *sachem*. The following table gives the name of each of the thirteen family groups on Long Island and the area in which it lived. Undoubtedly you will recognize many of these Indian tribes as names of places on Long Island today.

Name of Family Group	*Territory Inhabited*
Canarsie Indians	Brooklyn and part of Queens
Rockaway Indians	Queens and southern part of Hempstead Township
Merrick Indians	From Rockville Centre to west line of Oyster Bay Township
Massapequa Indians	From Fort Neck to west line of Town of Islip
Secatoag Indians	East of Massapequa to Patchogue
Patchoag Indians	From Patchogue to Canoe Place
Shinnecock Indians	From Canoe Place to East Hampton
Montauk Indians	Montauk Peninsula and Gardiners Island
Nissequogue Indians	Around Stony Point
Matinecock Indians	Flushing to Smithtown
Seatauket Indians	From Stony Brook to Wading River
Corchaug Indians	From Wading River to Orient Point
Manhasset Indians	Shelter Island

The Long Island Indians feared the more warlike Indians across the water such as the Pequots and the Narragansetts. These mainland tribes at one time or another claimed lordship over the Island Indians and demanded tribute. Indians from Connecticut and Massachusetts often crossed the Sound in large dugout canoes, each capable of holding from 60 to 80 warriors. They would attack the natives of Long Island and carry some of them off for ransom. In order to keep peace with their enemies, the Long Island Indians paid yearly tribute in the form of wampum and dried clams. One year, upon the advice of the Dutch settlers, the Long Island Indians refused to make their payment to the Mohawks, a strong upstate Iroquois tribe. They soon regretted this. The Mohawks swooped down the Hudson Valley, invaded Long Island and almost destroyed the Canarsies.

For further security, the Indians of eastern Long Island banded together under the leadership of the Montauks. Of the thirteen tribes, the Montauks were probably the most powerful. They were the best fighters and they had fortified their peninsula against invasion. At the time of the coming of the white man, their chief, Wyandanch, was called the "Grand Sachem of Paumanok." It was he who kept the Indians of Long Island friendly to the English when they settled here. In spite of many urgings on the part of the Narragansetts of New England to declare war on Europeans, he firmly refused to do so, thus saving the settlers of Long Island much hardship and suffering.

About 1650, the tribes on western Long Island united under one head. Tackapousha, sachem of the Massapequas, was elected to lead this western confederacy. The Tackapousha Reserve at Seaford, devoted to the conservation of wild life on Long Island, is named after this chief. The confederacy which he headed included the Massapequas, the Merricks, the Canarsies, the Secatoags, the Rockaways and the Matinecocks. Many of the early land transfers and peace treaties between Indians and whites bear Tackapousha's mark upon them.

INDIAN LIFE ON LONG ISLAND

The Indians living on Long Island were prosperous. Nature had provided this area with ample food. The Long Island Indians were farmers, fishermen and hunters. Maize (corn) grew well then, as it does today. Along with beans, maize was a chief Indian crop. The maize was ground into a rough flour by pounding it in a hollowed log with a wooden club called a pestle. Then it was mixed with water and baked in hot ashes to make a cake called Indian bread.

Wild life was plentiful. For the hunter there was deer, bear, raccoon, turkey, quail, partridge, geese and duck. Many of the Indian camp sites were pitched where a fresh water stream met a salt water inlet. It was here that seafood was most plentiful. To be found were oysters, clams, scallops, lobsters, crabs, and the many kinds of fish that we have today—bluefish, flounders, herring, bass and others. The Indians were expert fishermen, catching the fish with hook, harpoon, bow and arrow, gill net and seine. They were even so bold as to attack the whales which sometimes came close to the coast. With all this food the Long Island Indians seldom went hungry.

THE LONG ISLAND INDIANS BUILT THEIR WIGWAMS IN A DOME SHAPE
The above model in the American Museum of Natural History in New York City shows a wigwam during construction. Note that the framework is covered over, or thatched, with grass.

Their houses were simple and crude. Many of them were built in a dome shape about ten to twenty feet in diameter and thatched over with grass. A hole was left in the center for smoke to escape. The edges of the hole were covered with clay to prevent the roof from burning. The doorway was an arched pole over which a curtain of skin might be hung.

Inside this wigwam an elevated bench ran around the sides under which the Indian stored his goods. This bench acted as a bed, a table and a seat. The fireplace was in the center, beneath the hole in the roof. Often the wigwam was filled with smoke.

The Indians made their canoes by digging out tree trunks; they strung their bows with the sinews of animals; arrow points were made from chipped stone, a deer's antlers and shells. Their tools and utensils were rough. They made crude hammers, knives, spear heads and scrapers from stone; fish hooks were cut from bone; and rope was made from bark fiber.

The Long Island Indians did not develop pottery making into an art, as did the southwestern Indians. Long Island Indians used the coil method, that is, they built up their vessel by winding a coil of clay in layers, smoothing it out as they shaped the pot. Usually the pottery was pointed on the bottom so that it could be rested between rocks. While the clay was still soft, some clumsy attempt was made to decorate it by making impressions upon the sides with a scallop shell, or by drawing short lines across it with a pointed stick. Then the clay would be baked to harden it.

Other common household articles included spoons, fashioned from the dry shells of gourds, small baskets for holding the maize, and tiny clay pipes about large enough to hold a thimblefull of tobacco.

The Indian's dress varied with the season. During the cold weather he covered the upper part of his body with robes of dressed deer skin, or of wolf, wildcat and bear fur. With his soft moccasins he was able to tread noiselessly through the forest. In the warm months his clothes looked very much like our modern summer wear. He wore a breach clout, a garment which served the same purpose as our popular beach shorts do today.

The men shaved their heads using clam shell razors and tweezers. They left a short stiff line of hair, called a "roach," standing in the middle from the forehead to the neck. A scalplock was left hanging in the back with which the Indians defied their enemies, taunting to come and take it, if they could. The women, on the other hand, plaited their black hair into long braids, two braids if unmarried and one braid if wed.

Small children were bound to a stiff board, a cradle-like affair which was hung on a tree or some other convenient spot while the mother busied herself. Thus children were kept out of mischief until able to walk.

INDIANS AND SHELLFISH

Clams, oysters and other shellfish considerably influenced the lives of the Long Island Indians. The white men, who later inhabited the island, found large piles of shells marking the sites of ancient Indian villages. Some of these shell heaps measure as much as four feet in depth and several acres in area. The size of the heap depended upon the length of time the Indian tribe camped at a particular spot and upon the number of Indians in the tribe. The Long Island farmer has discovered that when these shells are ground they make excellent fertilizer.

Oysters, clams and crabs formed a large part of the Indians* food. Indeed, one colonial Dutchman joked, "If oysters had legs, Indians would starve."

In addition, the shell could be used for many purposes. If properly shaped, it served as a drinking cup. Arrowpoints were sometimes cut from sea shells. In making pottery, shells were crushed and mixed with the clay to act as a reinforcement. Flat shells were pierced with holes and worn as pendants suspended from the neck. Indian graves were often lined with shells. But the most interesting use of sea shells was for making wampum.

The word *wampum* comes from the early New Englander's interpretation of the Algonquian word "wampomeag," meaning "a string of shells." Another word for wampum is seawan, the Indian name for shell money.

In manufacturing wampum, the Indian made shell beads by cutting sea shells into small pieces and drilling a hole through the center of each piece. Then the shell beads were rubbed smooth and round on a large stone until a uniform size was attained, usually one quarter of an inch in length and one eighth of an inch in diameter.

These beads were strung on the sinews of small animals or on twisted threads made from the inner bark of the elm tree. Sometimes they were used for decorating belts, often seven beads wide, ranging from two to six feet in length. You may see some excellent examples of this work at the American Museum of Natural History in New York City.

Since all this work was done by hand, it took a long time and considerable skill. Therefore, it was assigned to the women of the tribe, whose skillful hands were accustomed to the delicate operations of bead making. White and black beads were used to make designs in the belt. The white bead came from conch shells, and the black came from the relatively scarce purple inside of the quahaug or hard clam.

It took much time and effort to make these belts. For this reason, wampum was considered precious by the Indians. It was often used as money for buying and selling things just as we use dollar bills today.

Not only was wampum used as money among the Indians, but the first white men copied this practice, using it as a medium of exchange among themselves as well as with the Indians. In trading, wampum was used either in strings or as loose beads. The black beads were worth twice the value of the white ones. Six white ones, or three black ones, were equal to an English penny.

By the string, wampum was measured in fathoms, a fathom being the distance between the tip of the little finger and the elbow. The settlers sometimes accused the Indians of using men who had short arms in measuring these fathoms when it was to their advantage in trading; or long arms as the case might be. So widespread was the use of wampum among the early whites, that it was accepted for payment of taxes, or to pay court fees. Nor was it unusual to find wampum in the church collection plate.

Wampum was also employed by the Indians along with the transmission of messages. A message which was sent without a belt was considered an "empty word" and little attention was paid to it.

INDIAN WOMAN MAKING WAMPUM

Wampum was made by cutting shells into small pieces and drilling holes through the pieces to form beads which were then used as money or for making belts.

The color of the beads had special meaning, with white beads representing peace, health and harmony, while dark beads told of death, sorrow or hostility. Beads dyed red meant war.

Besides these practical uses for wampum, it was worn as an article of adornment, being worked into dresses and belts. Bracelets, necklaces and earrings were made of it. Nowhere was wampum as well made as on Long Island.

Indeed it was possession of this wealth which brought dangers to the Long Island Indian. Thus, the more powerful tribes of the mainland forced our Indians to pay them wampum tribute in increasing amounts. If they failed to do so, they were soon raided. Hence, in order to escape punishment, the Long Island Indians were kept busy making more and more wampum to pay to their enemies across the water.

INDIANS AND WHITE MEN

The white man's relations with the Indians on Long Island got off to a good start in the person of the Englishman, Lion Gardiner. The story goes that when Wyandanch's daughter was being married, the wedding feast was halted by a band of raiding Narragansetts. They killed the bridegroom, captured the bride and carried her off to the mainland. Lion Gardiner offered his service to the mourning Montauk chief to rescue the girl. Through his efforts, a ransom was arranged, and the daughter was returned to her father. Wyandanch was ever grateful for Gardiner's aid. To express his appreciation, Wyandanch gave him some land in what is now Smithtown. This event built a lasting friendship between the Indians and the white men.

In general, the English who settled eastern Long Island had little trouble with the Indians. They were wise enough to pay the Indians for the land upon which they settled. While these payments were small, and later the white man would be accused of cheating, at the time the red man felt he was receiving something in exchange for his hunting grounds. For example, read the following Indian deed drawn up in 1648 between several Indian sachems and the English settlers at East Hampton. Decide for yourself why the Indians might regard Englishmen as being fair. In exchange for a large grant of territory the Indians received, ". . . twentie Coates, twentie-four looking-glasses, twentie-four hoes, twentie-four knives, One hundred muges . . ." Also, the Indians kept certain rights on this territory, ". . . Libertie, freely to fish in any or all the cricks and ponds, and hunt up and downe in the woods . . . Likewise, they are to have the fynns and tails of all such whales as shall be cast upp. . . (and) liberties to fish in all convenient places, for shells to make wampum. . ."

The English, therefore, were trusted by the Indians. The Indians taught the English settlers how to plant corn, showed them where the best fishing places were, how to tread for clams and how to attack the whales offshore.

The only battle between the Indians and the English on Long Island is said to have been fought at Fort Neck, near Massapequa, around 1653. We are not

THIS BRONZE INDIAN NOW STANDS
IN FRONT OF AN ANTIQUE SHOP
ON LONG ISLAND
The Indians on eastern Long Island
remained friendly with the early
English settlers and taught them how
to plant corn.

quite sure of the date. The Massapequa Indians had fortified this place and seemed to be making warlike preparations against the whites. Therefore, a band of English and Dutch colonists, under the leadership of Captain John Underhill, attacked and defeated them, killing one hundred Indians with the loss of only two or three of his men.

Hostilities ceased with a treaty signed between Tackapousha and the Dutch Government, which at that time claimed this territory. The treaty read:

"Articles of agreement, Betwixt the Government of ye New Netherlands and Tackapousha, Mch ye 12th, 1656

(I) That all injuries passed in the time of the Governor's predecessors shall be forgiven and forgotten since ye year 1645 and never be remembered. . . That the inhabitants of Hemsteede, according to their patent shall enjoy their purchase without mollestation from ye Sachem or his people. . . And the Governor doth promise for himself and all his people to live in peace with the sd. sachem and all his people."

As a consequence, except for a few incidents between individual Indians and colonists, the English were never really threatened again.

With the Dutch it was a different story. The people of New Netherlands—the Dutch—had settled western Long Island. The Dutch regarded the Indians with contempt and refused to recognize any Indian rights. The Indians were treated as slaves and were forced to pay high taxes. The red man was seldom paid for his land. There were even some times when the Dutch cruelly murdered them. To make matters worse, the Dutch gave the Indians firearms and rum in exchange for furs and wampum. As a result, it is not surprising that the Indians on the western part of the Island banded together and turned the guns against the Dutch.

Warfare broke out when some Dutch citizens of Flatlands attacked a band of Merricks, killing several Indians and stealing two wagonloads of corn. This injury started a fight which was to continue on and off until the English took control of the whole of New York, including western Long Island.

DISAPPEARANCE OF THE LONG ISLAND INDIAN

In less than a hundred years after the first white man settled on Long Island, there were scarcely any Indians left. By 1741, only four hundred were living on the island and these had lost their Indian ways. By the time of the Revolutionary War, the Indian was a rarity on Paumonok.

There are several reasons for the rapid disappearance of the Long Island Indian. First, there was the smallpox epidemic. The white man brought his diseases to the New World. In 1658, a smallpox epidemic broke out. This disease is said to have killed two-thirds of the natives.

INDIANS SOMETIMES ATTACKED THE DUTCH SETTLEMENTS ON WESTERN LONG ISLAND

Note the Dutch door that could open the top and remain closed at the botto for protection.

Also, as the colonists took over more and more of the land, extending their farms and clearings, the wild animals were driven away. Game became scarce and difficult to obtain. The Indians who preferred to live the Indian way of life and not the white man's, were forced to migrate to the mainland, seeking better hunting grounds. A few went as far as Wisconsin. Of those who remained behind, some became sailors, others went out with the whaling ships, and still others enlisted in the militia to fight the colonists' wars.

Also, the Indians lost their land. For example, in 1879 a white man persuaded some of the Montauk Indians to sell 9,200 acres of their land in exchange for a yearly payment of $80 per person. Then the white man sold the land to other white men for the huge sum of $650,000! Later Montauk Indians believed they were cheated and have taken the matter to court to regain their tribal lands.

(Courtesy of Nassau County Historical Museum)

DUTCH RECEIVING TRIBUTE

The Indians are not completely gone from us today—though it would be difficult for us to associate them with their ancestors. A few live mixed with the general population near East Hampton. Others, about four hundred, live on two small Long Island Indian reservations, the Poosepatuck Indian Reservation at Mastic and the Shinnecock Indian Reservation near Southampton. The land on these reservations is owned by the whole group, not by individuals.

The inhabitants do not especially look like "red men." It is hard to find a pure bred Indian because they have intermarried with both whites and blacks. Before the Civil War some of the escaped Negro slaves from the South came to live on Long Island. They intermarried with the few Indians who were left so that the Indians living on the reservations today may have more Negro blood than Indian blood.

Their habits and dress are much like those of any American. They work at jobs, much as everyone does and commute back and forth to the reservation. Some go to church. They have American names such as Lois Hunter who, up till 1975, when she died, was princess of the Shinnecock Indians.

Recently the Indians at Shinnecock have brought back some of the old customs. Once a year a pow-wow is held to which the whites are invited. During this celebration, Long Island Indians become hosts to Indians from other parts of the United States. Colorful Indian costumes, ceremonial dances and Indian handcrafts are displayed.

Today the Long Island Indians are best remembered by their interesting names. There is not a township on the map which does not have its Indian place names; names like Ronkonkoma, Copaigue, Massapequa, Rockaway, Setauket and Manhasset; names which have a melody—and when translated into our language have a poetry, too. Following is a list of places having Indian names together with the English translation:

>   Amagansett — the neighborhood of the fishing place
>   Massapequa — I have drunk enough or the great water land
>   Speonk — high land near water
>   Canarsie — at the fenced place
>   Rockaway — at the sandy place
>   Merrick — at the barren place
>   Matinecock — at the hilly place
>   Nissequogue — the clay or mud country
>   Setauket — land at the mouth of the river
>   Manhasset — an island sheltered by islands
>   Shinnecock — at the level place
>   Montauk — at the fortified place.

We have inherited Indian legends as well as Indian names. Their delightful stories have entertained many generations of boys and girls. A Long Island Indian tale tells about "The Devil and the Stones."

We all know how rocky the North Shore of Long Island is. It has always been rocky, and the Indians bemoaned this fact when they had to plant their corn. But, according to the Indian legend, in the early days Connecticut, just across the Sound, was smooth and fertile with not a stone in sight.

One day the Devil looked at Connecticut and decided he liked it. He thought that he would drive the Connecticut Indians away and live in such a lovely place himself. But when he tried to carry out his plan, the Connecticut Indians became so ferocious that he had to run away, jumping across the Sound from rock to rock to the safety of Long Island. He landed in the middle of the island at a place called Coram, and sat down and brooded.

The more he sulked about his bad fortune, the more angry he became. He became so angry that he went down to a spot near Cold Spring Harbor and gathered all the big rocks he could find. Then the Devil seized these stones and hurled them across the Sound into the green fields of Connecticut. To this day Connecticut has been every bit as rocky as Long Island. Thus, the Devil had his revenge.

The Indians said that they could prove that this story is true because they could show any unbeliever the print of the Devil's foot on the spot upon which he had stood to throw the stones.

SUMMARY

The so-called thirteen Indian tribes of Long Island were of Algonquian stock. The colonists found them peaceful and paying tribute to the Indians of the mainland. The sea provided them with a large part of their food and also with the raw materials necessary for making wampum. Wampum was the outstanding artistic product of the Long Island Indians. The Indians disappeared rapidly after the coming of the colonists, but their names and their legends remain to remind us of the original inhabitants of our Island.

WHAT WORDS ARE MISSING?

The Indians of western Long Island belonged to the (1) family of Algonquians while those on the eastern part belonged to the (2) family. The most commonly used name for Indian Long Island was (3). The name of the Indian tribe which inhabited the place where you live was (4). The Indian, who was known as the "Grand Sachem of Paumanack" at the time of the first English settlers, was (5). The Indian, who headed a confederacy on western Long Island in 1650, was (6). The Indians' wigwam as found on Long Island was usually covered with (7). The most famous Indian product on Long Island was (8). This could be used for various purposes such as (9, 10, and 11). The (12) had less trouble in getting along with the Indians than the (13) had. Two Indian reservations found on Long Island today are (14) and (15). We have inherited (16) and (17) to remind us of the original inhabitants of Long Island.

CHAPTER THINKING

1. The Long Island Indians were cowards for not being more warlike. Is this true? Give reasons for your answer.

2. Explain why wampum became a very important medium of exchange.

3. Is it possible for Long Island Indians today to live the old way of Indian life? Explain your answer.

ACTIVITIES

1. Draw an Indian map of Long Island showing the areas occupied by each of the thirteen tribes.

2. Construct a model of an Indian wigwam.

3. Make your own wampum belt using colored drinking straws or cylindrical beads.

4. Visit a museum that has a Long Island Indian display and tell what you see to your class.

HUDSON'S MEN LANDED ON LONG ISLAND
IN 1609

CHAPTER 3

Long Island Under Colonial Rule

On September 4, 1609, an Englishman by the name of Henry Hudson anchored his tiny vessel, the *Half Moon*, off the coast of Long Island. Hudson had been sent by the Dutch East India Company to find a new sea route to China. Thinking that what is now Jamaica Bay might be the passage, he attempted to sail through Rockaway Inlet to the water beyond. But the sand bars and the shallow water which blocked the entrance forced him to turn back.

Instead, Hudson landed some men near Coney Island to look over the situation. They were greatly impressed with this land, "Full of great tall oaks, and the land as pleasant to see with grass and flowers as ever they had seen, and very sweet smells came from them." Unfortunately, the excursion ended sadly, for, somehow one of the Englishmen insulted the Indians who came to greet him. A fight broke out in which the Englishman, John Colman, was killed. His comrades carried him away. So Hudson's sailors were the first white men to put foot on Long Island and fight the first battle between Indians and whites on Long Island. This was not a very good beginning.

But Hudson was not the first white man to see Long Island. We are not quite certain who should get credit for this. In 1498, more than a hundred years before Hudson's voyage, John Cabot, sailing for the English, explored the Atlantic Coast of North America and probably sighted Long Island at that time. This voyage laid the basis for the English claim to all North America, Long Island included—a claim over which England was to fight during the next three hundred years. Also, Giovanni Verrazano, another sea captain sailing for the English, saw Long Island when he anchored in New York Bay in 1524 and later sailed eastward along its coast. The long, graceful bridge found near that spot where he anchored in New York Bay is named after him. Furthermore, there is some reason to believe that the Vikings sighted Long Island as early as the year 1000.

Nevertheless, we give great importance to Henry Hudson's voyage because his explorations led directly to the settlement of what is now New York State. It brought about Dutch rule over New Netherlands, of which Long Island was a part, and thus stamped the Dutch character on western Long Island during colonial times.

DUTCH EXPLORATION AND COLONIZATION

In 1614, five years after Hudson's discovery, Adrian Block sailed into New York Bay. He was ordered by the Dutch to establish a fur trading post and engage in trade with the Indians. This he did on Manhattan Island and, later, when shipwrecked, he built another small ship called the *Onrust* (Restless).

With this boat Block continued his explorations. They took him through the East River and into Long Island Sound. He sailed eastward as far as Block Island, which he named after himself. In making this trip, Block discovered that Long Island was not part of the mainland, a fact which had not been established up to that time. He drew a map to show that Long Island was really an island.

In the beginning, the Dutch paid little attention to Long Island. When New Netherlands was first colonized, the Dutch concentrated their settlements in New Jersey and along the Hudson River. With all these lands open to settlement, it is no wonder that they overlooked Long Island, although they considered it part of their territory. Wouter Van Twiller, one of the Dutch governors, acquired some 7,600 acres in what is now Brooklyn for the purpose of making a handsome profit by reselling land to settlers. But it was not until the 1630's that individual Dutchmen began to move across the East River from New Amsterdam to establish farms on Lange Eylandt, as they called it.

The Dutch proceeded to cultivate "bouweries," their word for farms, and develop little villages. Five such villages were organized on western Long Island before the conquest of the English. Consequently, the English called this territory "the Five Dutch Towns." The towns were Midwout (Flatbush), Amersfoort (Flatlands), Breucklen, New Utrecht and Bushwick. Bruijkleen was the name given by the Dutch to all of their colony on Long Island.

The name Bruijkleen has an interesting history. In order to get colonists to come to New Netherlands, the Dutch West India Company offered a free piece of land to any pioneer who settled in the wilderness and cultivated the land for ten years, giving one tenth of the produce from the land during this time to the

Company. At the end of the ten year period, the settler was to receive full title to the land. Long Island was set aside as the land to be given to these settlers. Hence, it was called Bruijkleen, which means "free loan" land in Dutch. Later, the English called this territory Brookland, which is their version of Bruijkleen. Today it is Brooklyn.

In addition to the community of the Five Dutch Towns, the Dutch laid claim to the eastern part of Long Island. The English based their claim of ownership upon the explorations of John Cabot and upon the fact that several English towns were already established in this territory by colonists from Connecticut.

One would think that with all the land available for colonization, scant attention would be paid to Long Island. However, the Dutch had learned that Long Island was a valuable asset. With this territory in their hands, they had a monopoly over the Indian manufacture of wampum. By taxing the Long Island Indians in wampum, they thus secured this Indian form of money to be used in the valuable beaver skin trade with the Indians in northern New York.

The dispute over Long Island between the English and the Dutch was temporarily settled in 1650 at Hartford, Connecticut, when Peter Stuyvesant, the Dutch Governor, compromised with the English. The Dutch were in no position to enforce their claims, for the English were far more numerous in the New World. Furthermore, the Dutch West India Company would not give Stuyvesant enough money to set up proper fortifications. So the Dutch Governor had to swallow his pride and agree to the English terms. Long Island was divided by a line drawn south from Oyster Bay. All land to the west was kept by the Dutch while the land to the east was given to the English. Thus the Dutch retained the territory which was later to form the counties of Kings (Brooklyn), Queens and Nassau.

ENGLISH COLONISTS IN DUTCH TERRITORY

The Dutch were not so successful as the English had been in getting colonists to come to the New World. At home, the average Dutchman was satisfied with his lot and, therefore, less anxious than other Europeans to leave their homeland. Consequently, the Netherlands Government permitted foreigners to settle in New Netherlands and brought Negroes from Africa. The Europeans were allowed to practice their own religion and customs. In some cases they elected their own officials, providing they recognized the Dutch laws. Thus it was that several groups of English settlers petitioned the Dutch Governor to set up towns in Dutch territory on Long Island. Permission was granted.

Hempstead was the first and probably the most famous of these English towns in Dutch territory. In 1643, the Reverend Richard Denton of Stamford, Connecticut, seeking a better place for his congregation sent Robert Fordham and John Carman across the Sound to buy some land from the Indians.

They met Tackapousha, the Indian sachem, and entered into an agreement with him to buy most of the land of what is now the Town of Hempstead. In

(Courtesy of Nassau County Historical Muse

HEMPSTEAD PURCHASE, 1643

1644, upon receiving a patent (permission) from the Dutch Governor Kieft, Reverend Denton and his flock journeyed from Stamford to build their new homes on the Hempstead Plains. They agreed to pay taxes to the Dutch and to respect Dutch rule, but in all other respects Hempstead was strictly an English town from its very beginning.

Other English towns established in Dutch territory were Newtown, Flushing, Jamaica in Queens, and Gravesend in Brooklyn. Gravesend is interesting to us because of Lady Deborah Moody, the only woman to have received a grant of land on Long Island during colonial times. After a stormy career in England and later in Massachusetts, she and her followers went to Long Island in search of religious freedom. The Dutch permitted her to settle at Gravesend.

THE DUTCH WEST INDIA COMPANY

Dutch rule really meant rule by the Dutch West India Company. In the 1600's the people of the Netherlands were traders and merchants. Their city of Amsterdam was the greatest port in the world. Their ships covered the globe.

Some of their business men organized the Dutch West India Company in 1621 to carry on trade with the lands discovered in the New World. This company was given the right by the Netherlands Government to trade with and colonize West Africa and any place in the Americas from the Strait of Magellan to the farthest north regions.

The Government permitted the Dutch West India Company to settle any lands to which they could lay claim; to erect their own forts; to declare war or peace as they saw fit; to administer justice, having the right to throw a man into jail in their colonies; to appoint their own governors and in general to have absolute control over any of the places and people in its territory. Indeed, the settlers referred to the Directors of the Dutch West India Company as "Their High Mightinesses." So it was the Dutch West India Company, and not the Dutch Government, which ruled New Netherlands—and western Long Island.

The situation was not a happy one. The colonists came to America to gain the freedom and prosperity which were so often denied to them at home. On the other hand, the Dutch West India Company owners were mainly interested in making money on their investment. They were more concerned with the profitable beaver trade in the norther part of the colony than with the welfare of the colonists. Therefore, when the Company, through its various governors, attempted to tax the colonists heavily and restrict their trade for the benefit of the owners, the colonists became discontented.

As a result, the Dutch, even more than the English on Long Island, resented the interference of the Dutch West India Company. Instead of doing all trading through the port of New Amsterdam, as they were required, they smuggled goods in and out of the sheltered coves to avoid paying the tax demanded by the Company for all trade carried on in the colony.

Nor did the early Dutch settlers approve of the high-handed methods of some of the governors who acted like dictators. The last Dutch Governor, Peter Stuyvesant, while an efficient man, was the most autocratic of them all. During the eighteen years of his term of office, he constantly quarreled with the colonists, because he always did as he pleased.

Stuyvesant was very strict in enforcing the rules of the Company. At first the Dutch officials had been tolerant about religion, but Stuyvesant began to banish people who openly practiced a faith different from that of the Dutch Reformed Church. He went so far as to appoint ministers and tell them what to preach in their sermons. Also, whereas the English towns had been allowed a large amount of self-government, he began to take that privilege away.

These acts, however, did not go unchallenged. In 1653, delegates from four Dutch and four English towns on Long Island met in New Amsterdam. They drew up a protest against Stuyvesant and his methods. They complained of his dictatorial manner and insisted on their right to elect their own town officials and ministers.

Then the Quakers of Flushing drew up a protest in 1657. Stuyvesant had been particularly hard on the Quakers who had settled on Long Island. He forbade this religious group to hold meetings in their town of Flushing. Because of these restrictions, the townsfolk of Flushing signed a paper which became known as the Flushing Remonstrance. In it they said that Peter Stuyvesant had no right to deny them freedom of religion. The Remonstrance claimed rights for Christians, Jews and for ordinary citizens. It has been called the "first American Declaration of Independence."

The Dutch West India Company scolded Governor Stuyvesant for stirring up so much trouble over the Quakers. The Company wrote a letter from Amsterdam to Stuyvesant on April 6, 1663, that said: ". . . you ought rather to encourage rather than check the population of the colony. The *consciences* of men ought to be *free* and *unshackled* so long as they continue moderate, peaceable, inoffensive and not hostile to the government. . . (T)he *oppressed* and *persecuted* from every country have found among us an *asylum* from distress. *Follow in the same steps and you will be blessed.*"

Soon there was other cause for trouble. First, Captain John Underhill, the famous Indian fighter, went through the English towns stirring the people to rebel against the Dutch. In 1653, he raised the English flag in Hempstead but was promptly arrested and sent away.

Then in 1662, Connecticut received a new charter from the King of England. On the basis of this charter, it claimed ownership over all Long Island. A representative was sent to Long Island to inform the people that they were to cease paying taxes to the Dutch and henceforth were to consider themselves subjects of the colony of Connecticut.

Finally, in 1664, an English adventurer by the name of Captain John Scott spread the word that the Duke of York owned Long Island. He put himself at the head of 150 men and proceeded to conquer the Dutch towns on Long Island, proclaiming Charles II, the English king, as ruler. He proclaimed himself "President of Long Island." Peter Stuyvesant could do little to oppose him since he did not have sufficient military force to stop Scott.

ENGLAND CONQUERS NEW NETHERLANDS

In the meantime, events were taking place in England which would settle the fate of Long Island for some time to come. On the basis of Cabot's explorations, England had always claimed the Atlantic seaboard as her own. The English looked upon the Dutch settlers as "squatters," having no right to the territory they inhabited.

In 1635, King Charles the First granted to the Earl of Sterling a large tract of land in America, including "Long Island and Islands adjacent." However, the Earl of Sterling made no attempt to take western Long Island. Then, in 1664, Charles II gave his brother, the Duke of York, the Dutch colony of New Netherlands, totally disregarding the claims of the Dutch. The grant included Long Island.

The Duke lost no time in preparing a fleet to take possession of the colony. That very same year three English ships and 450 troops under the command of Colonel Richard Nicolls appeared off the coast of New Netherlands. Nicolls landed some troops at Gravesend, calling for submission of Long Island to his authority. The troops marched to the ferry at Breucklen where they were met by volunteers from Long Island and New England. The fleet sailed up the harbor and anchored in front of the fort at New Amsterdam.

Peter Stuyvesant had no choice. He had few soldiers and only twenty cannon. The colonists would not fight for him. They were tired of the Dutch dictatorial rule and thought that the English would allow them the freedom they had sought. So New Netherlands, including Long Island, became New York under English control.

THE DUTCH GOVERNOR, PETER STUYVESANT, SURRENDERED NEW NETHERLANDS TO THE ENGLISH IN 1664.

DUTCH CONTRIBUTIONS

The Dutch left a lasting impression upon the area. You already know of the Dutch names on western Long Island such as New Utrecht, Bushwick, Brooklyn and others. Their houses are copied by us today. One style of architecture on Long Island is the Dutch farmhouse type, with roof curving over a wide porch and front door cut in half so that one may open the top without opening the bottom.

The Dutch brought a respect for cleanliness with them, for the Dutch are a very neat people. Everything was spotlessly clean in their homes; the copperware shone, the linen was a crisp white, and they sprinkled their floors with clean white sand, working designs into it with a broom. Pity the poor Dutch husband who forgot to take off his muddy boots at the door upon entering his wife's tidy kitchen.

TYPICAL DUTCH FARMHOUSE

The people of The Netherlands introduced into the New World many new and delightful customs which have become part of American life. The idea of Santa Claus was started by them, and they were the first ones to hang stockings over the fireplace on Christmas Eve. They liked to eat good things and on their frequent holidays they baked pancakes, waffles, cookies and other sweets. They loved flowers and brought tulip bulbs to America from their native Holland. The descendants of these Dutch colonists played an important part in the history of Long Island. President Theodore Roosevelt was a famous Long Islander of Dutch descent.

EARLY ENGLISH SETTLEMENT OF LONG ISLAND

By 1664, all Long Island was under English rule. We have already seen how the English came to possess the Island through their claim based on the explorations of John Cabot, and later through the grants made to the Earl of Sterling and the Duke of York. We learned that, even while western Long Island was Dutch territory, several English towns had been firmly established in this area. Let us now turn our attention to the happenings on eastern Long Island during these times and follow English colonization there.

English settlement of eastern Long Island started in 1639 with Lion Gardiner's purchase from the Earl of Sterling of what is now Gardiner's Island. Gardiner was an English officer and engineer who had been commissioned to build fortifications for the colonists of Connecticut. Upon completing his work, he moved with his wife and children to the island which now bears his name. Thus, he and his family became the first white inhabitants of eastern Long Island. To this day Gardiner's Island is owned by the Gardiner family.

Southampton was settled in 1640. Eight Englishmen from Lynn, Massachusetts, landed there after having bought the place from the Earl of Sterling's land agent, James Farret. The Indians proved to be friendly, and the colonists entered into an agreement with them to purchase the land "in consideration of sixteen coats already received and also three score bushels of Indian corn. . . and further in consideration that they, the above named English, shall defend us, the said Indians, from the unjust violence of whatever Indians shall illegally assail us."

For the most part, this was the manner of settlement that the English practiced. First they sent a scouting party out to choose the place of settlement. Then, as their law required, they bought it from the Indians. Then they had the deal approved by whatever Englishman had jurisdiction over the territory. Finally, from ten to thirty families would go out with all their belongings to inhabit the new place.

That same year, 1640, saw the settlement of Southold. This town was founded by a minister, John Youngs, who crossed the Sound from New Haven with his followers in search of a place to practice his religion. Later, some French Huguenots (French Protestants) joined Youngs in establishing the town of Southold.

Then, in rapid succession, small communities began to spring up all over Long Island. Among them was East Hampton, first known as Maidstone, on land bought from the Montauks. Huntington, Setauket and Brookhaven were settled in 1651, and in 1663 Major Richard Smith founded Smithtown.

The Smiths have a unique place in the history of Long Island. It is said that Richard Smith, the first Smith, bought all the land he could cover when riding between sunrise and sunset of the same day. He used a bull for this journey, and the place where he stopped to each lunch is still called "Bread and Cheese Hollow."

THIS STATUE IN SMITHTOWN WAS ERECTED IN HONOR OF RICHARD SMITH WHO FOUNDED SMITHTOWN
IN 1663

Soon there were many Smith families on Long Island. To tell one from the other, the early inhabitants called them by distinguishing names. Thus, there were the Bull-Smiths, so-called because Richard Smith rode a bull instead of a horse wherever he went. The Rock-Smiths were so called because they erected their house against a large rock. The Blue-Smiths came by their name because their ancestor wore a blue coat all the time. The Weight-Smiths possessed the only set of weights and scales in the community. The Tangier-Smiths were so distinguished because Colonel William Smith had once been Governor of Tangier.

As a result of this rapid colonization, English towns soon dotted the Long Island countryside from Montauk Point to Gravesend. By 1664, when the

English took over control of all Long Island, the following important English towns existed:

Gravesend	Brookhaven
Newtown	Southold
Flushing	Southampton
Hempstead	East Hampton
Huntington	Jamaica

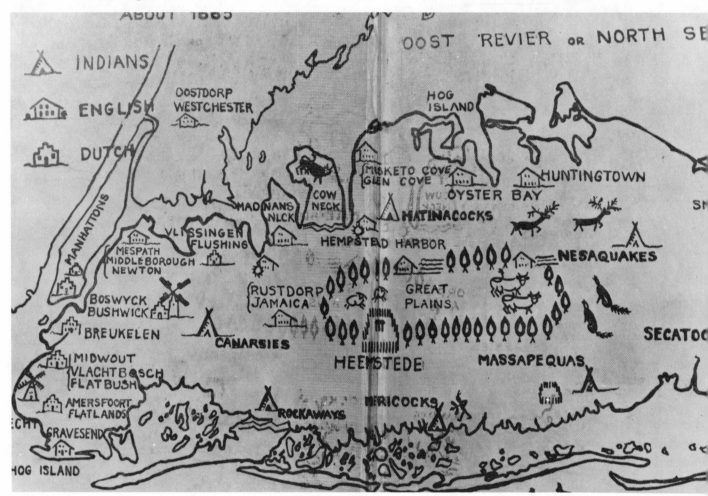

(Courtesy of Nassau County Historical Museum)

COLONIAL LONG ISLAND IN 1665

WHY THE ENGLISH CAME

The English did not come to the New World primarily to get rich on the fur trade, as had the Dutch. Many of them lacked the opportunity of making a good living back home, so they emigrated to America to cultivate farms and build homes in the wilderness. In contrast with the mother country, there was a chance in the New World to own land and to pass it on to their children.

OLD QUAKER MEETING HOUSE AT JERICHO

But an even more compelling reason for coming to America in these early days was the desire of the colonists to practice their own religion. In England the Church of England was the official church, and everyone was forced to support it. So these brave men and women came to America where the Church of England had no power, set up their own churches and elected their own ministers. Consequently, the English towns on Long Island were strongly religious. For quite some time, the church dominated affairs in these towns. Southold, especially, was a religious community. Here, the pastor was the leader of the colony, and the church was the government. The church was supported by a town tax, and only church members could vote at town meetings. Hempstead, too, was founded as a religious community when the Reverend Denton took his flock there.

Quakers, who had been severely persecuted elsewhere, found a refuge on Long Island. Westbury and Jericho were two towns settled by the Quakers. At these places you can see their meeting house still in use today. The Bowne House in Flushing is another Quaker landmark standing today. George Fox, the English founder of the Society of Friends as the Quakers are called, was a guest at the Bowne House. Thus, Long Island became a haven for conflicting religious faiths. While, occasionally, there was some persecution, it occurred much less than in most other sections of America.

ENGLISH LIFE ON LONG ISLAND

The early English settlers live a hard life at first. Those who inhabited eastern Long Island lived by themselves, and their only means of communication was by boat across the Sound to Connecticut. Since many of them came from Connecticut it was natural that they should have looked to that Colony for protection. Therefore, town after town on eastern Long Island allied itself with the Connecticut Government. Even when the Duke of York assumed control of Long Island, the eastern towns were reluctant to give up their ties with Connecticut.

The English colonists cleared the land and became farmers and cattleraisers. Later, they also became fishermen. Everyone had to work hard in order to survive the first years. The women took care of household chores; they did the cooking, the spinning, the sewing, the soap making, the nursing, and the raising of children, teaching the young ones how to read and write. The men labored outdoors, building houses and barns, clearing the land and farming, woodcutting, fishing, and raising livestock. Later on, some families bought one or two black slaves to help out and sometimes even Indians were made slaves. Freeport, Long Island, was called a "free port" because slave ships docked there to avoid paying the government tax on their human cargoes.

The houses on eastern Long Island were not like those of the Dutch. They were built without a porch, and they usually faced south, no matter how the road ran, to catch the warmth of the sun. As you can see, the colonists knew about solar heating, too! Many of them were built with two stories in the front, but with the roof slanted downward in the back so that it allowed room for only one story. Since they looked like the boxes in which salt had been stored in those days they were called "salt box" houses.

The people who lived closer to New York City had a better time of it and enjoyed more of the luxuries of life. Large manor houses were built, a few of which are standing today. Life was somewhat gayer on western Long Island, and there were parties and celebrations with horse racing at Jamaica in those early days.

What we owe to the English is too much to tell here. They gave us the language which we speak. Our tongue, which we might call "American," is really English with a great many new words and expressions added to it which are not used in England today. For example, we say *elevator* but the English say *lift* for the same thing; we say *gasoline*, the English say *petrol*; we say *baby carriage*, the English say *perambulator*; and there are many other differences.

TYPICAL "SALT BOX" HOUSE

Furthermore, many of our everyday habits are derived from the English. Our customs in marriage, religion, schooling and industry began in Great Britain. Of course, many of these customs were modified or changed because of the new conditions which the colonists were forced to face in the wild new land. But, nevertheless, we owe a great debt to Britain.

(Courtesy of Nassau County Historical Museum)

KITCHEN

SUMMARY

During the 1600's the Dutch settled on the western end of Long Island while the English settled on the eastern end. The Dutch claim to this territory rested upon the discoveries of Henry Hudson in 1609 while the English claim to ownership was based on John Cabot's explorations. The Dutch settlers were ruled by the Dutch West India Company which was mostly interested in the profitable beaver fur trade in the New York area. The English were chiefly small farmers and had settled on Long Island for religious reasons.

Up to 1664, ownership of Long Island was disputed by these two peoples. The dispute was settled by the conquest of New Netherlands by the Duke of York. Thereafter, Long Island grew as an English colony; older towns expanded and new ones were started. Long Island attracted settlers because, among other things, it had become a haven for people seeking religious freedom.

WHAT WORDS ARE MISSING?

Settlement of Long Island began after the exploration of (1) in 1609. The man who proved that Long Island is an island was (2). The English claimed Long Island on the basis of the voyages of (3). The Dutch settled on the (4) part of Long Island while the English settled on the (5) part. The Dutch permitted the English to settle in their territory in the town of (6). The ruling body for New Netherlands was (7). The strongest of the Dutch governors of New Netherlands was (8). Two Englishmen who had been granted Long Island by the King of England at different times were (9) and (10). New Netherlands was conquered by the English in the year (11). The first Englishman to settle eastern Long Island was (12). Two important reasons why the English settled on Long Island were (13) and (14). Houses that have two stories in the front and one story at the back as found during colonial times on Long Island are known as (15).

CHAPTER THINKING

1. Why was it more difficult for the Dutch to settle their colony than it was for the English?

2. Why is the year 1664 an important turning point in the history of Long Island?

3. Long Island is considered one of the birthplaces of freedom of religion in our country. Explain why this is so.

4. Do you think that the letter that the Dutch West India Company wrote to Peter Stuyvesant on April 6, 1663 (page 00) was fair? Explain your answer.

(Courtesy of Nassau County Historical Museur

ROCK HALL

ACTIVITIES

1. Draw a map of colonial Long Island showing:

   (a) Dutch and English territory.
   (b) Outstanding towns and dates of settlement.

2. Reports: Choose one of the following men and get some more information about him. Write a report to read to the class.

Henry Hudson	John Underhill
John Cabot	Peter Stuyvesant
Lion Gardiner	

3. Draw two pictures showing an early Dutch type house and an early English type house on Long Island.

4. Construct a model of a "salt box" house.

5. Visit a museum showing colonial exhibits of Long Island and report what you see to your class.

CHAPTER 4

Long Island Becomes Part of a Free Country

By 1770 Long Island was a well settled and important agricultural district of the colony of New York. It numbered about 30,000 people. Not only did the English own New York but they also ruled other American colonies up and down the Atlantic coast. Great Britain had become a powerful empire with colonies all over the world. Long Island was part of that empire.

Gradually, the American colonists, including Long Islanders, began to object to British rule and speak of freedom. At last, despite their close ties with the English people, the Americans revolted and a long war broke out. Let us see what the Revolutionary War did to Long Island.

CAUSES OF THE REVOLUTION

New Yorkers found that the English were not so liberal in granting self government as they first thought when the Dutch surrendered to a small English fleet in 1664. They experienced their first disappointment when Colonel Richard Nicolls, Governor of New York, summoned the Long Island towns to send representatives to a meeting at Hempstead in 1665 for the purpose of setting up a new government based upon English law.

Governor Nicolls announced to the assembled delegates a new set of laws, known as the Duke's Laws, which were to be used in governing the Colony. They provided for trial by jury and fair taxation methods, but they were lacking one very important provision dear to the hearts of the colonists. No self government was provided. The Governor had complete power and his word was law, so Long Islanders had their first cause to grumble about English rule.

Soon other events rose about which to complain. English laws were passed forbidding the colonies to trade directly with European countries or India. All goods must first go to England and from there be shipped on English ships to their destination.

This was very inconvenient for the Yankee shippers who wanted to trade with Spain or Portugal or some other country. They had to sell their products at a high price in order to meet the extra transportation costs if they wished to make a profit. Also, New York City was the port of entry for goods destined for Long Island. Here the British levied a tax on all shipping, which made the imported articles more expensive to buy.

As a result of these laws forbidding trade with European countries, some of the American merchants became smugglers. Long Island was a good place for smuggling operations. Ships could slip in and out of the little coves under the cover of darkness, thus escaping the payment of the duty charged at New York City.

So extensive were these operations that Long Island became known as Crooked Row. Lord Bellomont, one of the English governors of New York, wrote home that almost one third of the amount which entered New York came by way of smuggling on Long Island. It was estimated that the British were losing £12,000 a year in duties.

He further complained that it was difficult to hire revenue officers for duty on Long Island since it was considered a dangerous occupation. Occasionally British inspectors, or revenue officers, would tour the Island to detect any smuggler's goods. However, they received a very hostile reception from the local inhabitants and seldom were successful. Smuggling, and even piracy, was not looked upon as a terrible crime in those days, and more than one Long Islander became rich from this trade.

The English also interfered in the whaling industry when they put a ten per cent tax on all whale oil. This particularly hurt Long Islanders, because by this time whaling had become a profitable enterprise.

The story is told of Samuel Mulford, whaleman of East Hampton, who went to London to object to the restrictions on whaling. He had heard much about the thievery that took place on London streets, so he went there with fish hooks sewn in his pockets to catch the pickpockets. This caused such amusement among Londoners that he came to the attention of the authorities and thus secured an audience in Court to state his case. He won his point, and Long Islanders were allowed their full share of the whales they caught.

Repeatedly the Americans demanded a voice in Parliament, the English law-making body, but this was denied to them. Their affairs were run, to a large extent, not by themselves, but by the British Government, and they said, "No taxation with representation."

When a stamp tax was passed by the British Parliament, requiring that all legal documents bear stamps, they objected very strenuously. The British were forced to repeal the tax. Then a tax was put upon tea, but the Americans refused to pay it and threw the tea into the harbor.

Finally, in order to enforce the laws, King George III sent thousands of British troops to America and stationed them in the large cities. This angered the colonists. So they sent delegates to a Second Continental Congress in Philadelphia. Then on July 4, 1776, these representatives of the American colonies declared that from that day forward the American colonies would be independent of Great Britain. This was the famous Declaration of In-

TEA ACT DENOUNCED IN NEW YORK

(Courtesy of Nassau County Historical Museum)

dependence, signed by 56 Americans among whom was William Floyd, a native son of Long Island. *

How did Long Islanders feel about these developments? Were they in favor of independence and war or did they want the rule of Great Britain and peace? As in other parts of New York State, the people of Long Island were divided in their sentiments. Many of the inhabitants of Kings County were Dutch. They were more or less neutral, believing that this was not their quarrel, and they tried to keep out of trouble if possible. They could work with a rebel as well as a British officer without its bothering their consciences too much.

Many of the people of eastern Long Island were decidedly in favor of the Revolution and strongly supported it. For the most part, they were small farmers and fishermen who worked hard for a living. Men like these formed the backbone of the American Army. On the other hand, the people of what is now Queens and Nassau counties were split in their sympathies. Some supported the Americans. Many others, called Loyalists, supported the British. Some were neutral, hoping that the quarrel could be settled peaceably. Within a single family it was not strange in those times to find one member favoring the British while another favored the Americans. For example, William Floyd's

* Two more Long Islanders signed the Declaration of Independence but they did not have as strong a tie with Long Island as William Floyd had. They were Philip Livingston, who maintained a summer residence in Brooklyn, and Francis Lewis, who lived in Whitestone.

cousin was a staunch Loyalist. Many of those who were Loyalists, or Tories, helped the British in an active fashion. They would spy on the rebels and take their information to British officers. Some went to the extent of forming their own regiments to fight alongside of the British against the Patriots, as the rebels were called.

THE OUTBREAK OF THE REVOLUTIONARY WAR ON LONG ISLAND

When the war began, the people of New York formed a new and independent government. The English Governor, Tryon, and his friends were forced to flee to North Carolina. In 1775, the Provincial Congress, as the new government was called, summoned all New York counties to send delegates to it.

Many of the Long Island towns recognized this newly formed Congress immediately. Others refused to comply with the order, saying that the government was illegal. These latter towns drew up resolutions proclaiming their continued loyalty to the British king. Then, on November 7, 1775, an election was held in Jamaica to determine whether or not Queens County (at present the same territory as Queens and Nassau counties) would be represented in the Provincial Congress. The vote was 788 to 221 against sending a delegate. Therefore, Queens County remained unrepresented in the Provincial Congress throughout the war.

The results of the election in Queens County so enraged the members of the Provincial Congress that they decided to send a military expedition against the Loyalists of Long Island in order to disarm them and arrest their leaders. Laws were passed depriving them of many of their rights.

Colonel Heard, at the head of a small army, invaded Queens to force the Loyalists there to take an oath supporting the new government. Those who refused were imprisoned, their cattle slaughtered, and their property taken away, even their children were taken as hostages. Hundreds of Loyalists fled before the approaching army, hiding in the forests and swamps as best they could. There they stayed until the British regained control of Long Island in August, 1776.

THE BATTLE OF LONG ISLAND

The Battle of Long Island was the first big battle of the Revolutionary War. It was fought on Brooklyn Heights, an elevation which overlooks New York Harbor.

Upon learning that the British were sending a huge army and many warships to New York to win the war in one quick blow before the rebels had a chance to organize, the Americans began to make hasty preparations for battle. They fortified a hill in Brooklyn to protect New York City.

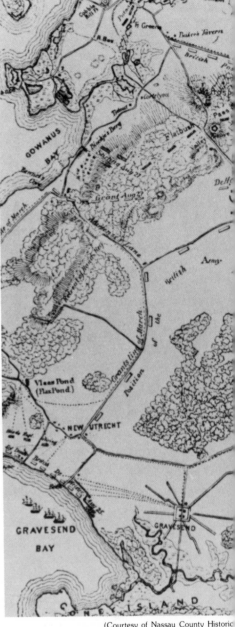

(Courtesy of Nassau County Historic

EARLY BROOKLYN BATTLE MAP

THE BATTLE OF LONG ISLAND WAS
THE FIRST BIG BATTLE OF THE
REVOLUTIONARY WAR

The British landed on Staten Island across the Bay. On August 22, 1776, they crossed the Bay to Long Island in flatboats, 20,000 strong, under the protection of guns from their own fleet at anchor. A fight took place in which the Americans, with their poor equipment, were no match for the enemy. The British and Hessian soldiers advanced while the Americans fell back. Unfortunately for the Patriots, soldiers in the right wing of the British Army discovered an unguarded pass to the Jamaica Road which led around the rear of the American Army. Quickly they took advantage of this and soon had the Americans trapped.

During the battle, one tremendous feat of bravery stands out on the American side. A regiment of Maryland soldiers, besieged on three sides by the enemy, held ground stubbornly, fighting off attack after attack in order to allow the rest of the Americans to escape. All but a handful of the courageous Marylanders were killed. A number of Negro soldiers also became heroes that day. They helped "preserve our army from capture."

When the day was over, it told a sad story for the Americans. The Army had suffered great losses in men and equipment. The soldiers were tired, dispirited and many were ready to quit. The English casualties were few. If ever there was a time to crush the rebellion with one blow, that was it. But the English general, Howe, failed to follow up his victory, saying that the soldiers had done enough for one day and the men should rest.

His brother, Lord Howe, admiral of the British fleet, was also slow in moving his ships up the East River. If he had done so, he could have prevented the Americans from escaping. Instead, during the night, the American Army had been silently transported across the River to the safety of Manhattan under cover of a thick fog—thus they lived to fight another day.

(Courtesy of Nassau County Historical Museum)

THE RETREAT FROM LONG ISLAND

In the meantime out on Long Island, General Nathaniel Woodhull was complying with orders issued by the Provincial Congress to drive all the cattle in Queens eastward out of reach of the invading British and to burn all other useful supplies. It has been estimated that at that time there were 100,000 horned cattle on Long Island and an even larger number of sheep—a rich prize for the British.

As he stood waiting in Hollis for further instructions, not knowing that the Americans had lost the battle, a party of British dragoons (cavalrymen) captured him and the thousands of cattle in his charge. His captors ordered him to say, "God save the King!" but General Woodhull said, "God save us all!" An angry British officer struck him with his sword. Woodhull died from the infection which later set in as a result of this sword wound.

AFTER THE BATTLE OF LONG ISLAND, THE AMERICAN ARMY ESCAPED BY ROWING ACROSS THE EAST RIVER

BRITISH PRISON SHIPS

The British soon had all Long Island under their control. Yankee soldiers and other rebellious subjects were quickly sent to the prison ships in Wallabout Bay. These ships were a disgrace to the British Navy. Imprisonment upon one of them was considered a death sentence.

The prison ships were old hulks once part of the British Navy but now considered unworthy for further sailing. Their masts were taken off and the ships made ready for prisoners. Living conditions on board were terrible. There was no light below the main deck, and the air was foul. The water had a bad taste. The prisoners were fed food not fit for human beings. One thousand prisoners were crowded into each ship. Under these conditions, diseases of every kind spread rapidly. It is said that each morning the British guards roused the prisoners by shouting down the hold, "Rebels, turn out your dead!" Many Americans died aboard the British prison ships anchored in Wallabout Bay.

BRITISH OCCUPATION OF LONG ISLAND

With the British occupation of Long Island, the Loyalists came out of hiding from the swamps and the woods. They welcomed their delivers and aided them in maintaining control. Loyalists from other parts of the country, where the rebels still held control, came to dwell on Long Island and the Patriots were driven into the swamps or to the safety of friendly Connecticut shores.

The Loyalists formed their own regiments to police Long Island. One was under the command of Oliver de Lancey. Another, stationed at Oyster Bay and known as the Queens Rangers, was commanded by Lieutenant Colonel John Graves Simcoe. The British and the Loyalist troops occupied Long Island until 1783.

During the occupation, Long Island became a supply depot for the British Army. Practically all firewood used by the British in New York came from Long Island. Thousands of cattle, sheep, hogs and poultry were either sold to the British or taken by them.

WHALEBOAT RAIDS

The Battle of Long Island did not end all warfare in this area. On the contrary, from time to time there were some very lively skirmishes between the British and the Americans. Long Island became a favorite raiding ground for Yankee whaleboat crews. They sneaked across the Sound from Connecticut and in lightning-like thrusts descended upon outlying parties of British soldiers or on whole villages to carry away supplies, capture prisoners and burn anything useful to the enemy.

The raid upon the British at Sag Harbor in 1777 was an especially daring one. Colonel Meigs of Connecticut, at the head of 170 men in 13 whaleboats, slipped across the Sound one night to land near Greenport. The boats were carried across the narrow strip of land of the North Fork and rowed across Peconic Bay. Then the men disembarked and cut through the woods behind Sag Harbor. They took the British completely by surprise. Ninety prisoners were captured. In addition, ten ships loaded with provisions for the British Army were burned, one ten gun ship destroyed and many supplies on shore burned.

In these raids influential Loyalists were kidnapped for ransom or to be exchanged for British-held American prisoners. Valuable articles were stolen. Unfortunately, at times the whaleboat men did not distinguish between friend and foe in their raids. After a while both sides in the struggle began to frown upon these raids because they had become mere thievery without any regard for the principles of the Revolution.

WASHINGTON'S SPIES

Spying was an important activity on Long Island. Setauket was the American spy center and from there information concerning the movements of the British was sent to General Washington. Among the outstanding spies were Nathan Hale, Robert Townsend and Abraham Woodhull.

Most of us know about Nathan Hale. He volunteered to cross the Sound from Connecticut to Long Island to report on the activities of the British. Unfortunately, he was captured and condemned to death by the British in New York. His dying words became famous: "I regret that I have only one life to lose for my country."

Until recently, however, little has been known of the other two spies, so well did they keep their secret.

Robert Townsend of Raynham Hall, Oyster Bay, whose house had become a British headquarters, posed as a reporter for the Royal Gazette, a British newspaper in New York City. In this position he received much information from British officers about British plans. He regularly sent messages in invisible ink to Abraham Woodhull in Setauket. Woodhull, in turn, would keep his eye on Nancy Strong's clothesline. When Nancy hung her wash in a certain way it

WHALEBOAT PRESERVED BY THE WHALING MUSEUM AT SAG HARBOR

NATHAN HALE SAID, "I REGRET THAT I HAVE BUT ONE LIFE TO LOSE FOR MY COUNTRY!"

meant that a messenger was waiting for Woodhull in one of six nearby creeks to take the information across the Sound to Connecticut. The clothesline code told Woodhull which creek to go to. For example, one message sent by Woodhull, whose spy name was "Culper Senior," read as follows: "There is about 300, most of them Hessians, at Brooklyn Ferry. 350 New Town, British; 1500 British Jamaica; 800 Yeagers, Flushing; 200 Jerico, most of them Dragoons; 400 foot, 70 Dragoons Oyster Bay . . . 100 troops this day in Smithtown collecting cattle, sheep, Boards, etc. . . ." This system of spying was used repeatedly throughout the whole war without discovery.

THE WAR ENDS

The war continued to be fought in other colonies until the Americans won a great victory at Yorktown, Virginia, in 1781. Then the British decided to wash their hads of the matter. In 1783, with the signing of the Treaty of Paris, the American colonies became free of Great Britain. The British soldiers left Long Island and many Loyalists went with them to Canada. More than one third of the population of Queens County was evacuated to Nova Scotia at the end of the Revolutionary War. Patriots, who had been dispossessed, returned to their homes and settled down to repair the damages of war. They were free Americans now, not English colonists.

OTHER PEOPLE ON LONG ISLAND

After the Revolutionary War since Long Island was a part of New York State it naturally became part of the new free country. The thirteen British-American colonies had become thirteen independent states of which New York was one. A Constitution was drawn up and in 1789 the thirteen states joined together to become the United States of America.

In the early 1800's Long Island grew slowly but beginning in 1830 the population shot upward. People of many different backgrounds besides Dutch and English began to settle here. They have all contributed to our history and prosperity. Earlier, the French Huguenots came from France to escape religious persecution. Many of these Protestants made their homes in Southold, Flushing and Bushwick. Another important group was the Negroes, mostly from West Africa. The blacks were forcibly shipped here in chains to become slaves. Before the Revolution slavery was permitted on Long Island and many prosperous farmers owned one or two slaves to work the fields and do the household chores. However, after the war a strong feeling against slavery developed. Long Island Quakers, in particular, condemned this cruel practice and urged everyone to free his slaves. Some slaveowners did this. For example, in 1788, Thomas Tredwell freed a slave as follows: "Be it known to all whom it may concern, that I Thomas Tredwell of Smithtown in the County of Suffolk Esquire, for and in consideration of the fidelity and past service of my negro man slave named Charles, aged about twenty six years, and set at liberty my said negro man slave named Charles, and I do hereby for myself my heirs,

FIGURINES OF THE REVOLUTIONA
WAR PERIOD.

VILLAGE OF HEMPSTEAD, 1890

executors and administrators absolutely relinquish and release all my right title property claim and demand, in and to the said Charles or any future service or services from him as a slave. . . ."

Finally, in 1828, New York passed a law making it illegal to own a slave in that state and, as a result, all slaves on Long Island were freed.

In the 1800's and 1900's more immigrants, as the settlers from overseas were now called, poured in to make their homes on Long Island. During the 1800's most of the immigrants came from the northern European countries such as Germany, Sweden, Norway and Ireland. These people did not come as the earlier settlers did, to carve out a home for themselves in the wilderness, because the wilderness in this part of the United States was gone. They came to get jobs. The Irish came because they could not grow enough food in their country. The potato crop, their main food, had failed. They came to America in the middle 1800's and helped build up our cities. Many Germans came because they could not get democratic rights in their native land. They journeyed to America because this country offered these rights to them.

The population of Long Island grew by leaps and bounds until the 1970's. In the late 1970's Long Island stopped growing. Following is a table showing the increase in population from 1790 to 1970:

POPULATION GROWTH OF LONG ISLAND

Year	Kings	Queens	Nassau*	Suffolk	Total
1790	4,495	16,014		16,440	36.949
1800	5,740	16,893		19,464	42,097
1810	8,303	19,336		21,113	48,752
1820	11,187	21,519		24,272	56,978
1830	20,535	22,460		26,780	69,775
1840	47,613	30,324		32,469	110,505
1850	138,882	36,833		36,922	212,637
1860	274,123	54,004		41,461	369,588
1870	419,907	73,798		46,762	540,467
1880	599,354	90,544		53,825	743,723
1890	838,547	128,059		62,491	929,097
1900	1,166,582	152,999	55,448	77,582	1,452,611
1910	1,634,351	284,041	83,930	96,138	2,098,460
1920	2,018,356	469,042	126,120	110,246	2,723,764
1930	2,560,401	1,079,129	303,053	161,055	4,103,638
1940	2,698,285	1,297,634	406,748	197,355	4,600,022
1950	2,720,238	1,546,316	665,746	272,359	5,304,659
1960	2,627,319	1,809,578	1,300,171	666,784	6,403,852
1970	2,602,612	1,987,174	1,428,833	1,127,630	7,145,054
1980	2,276,400	1,941,600	1,392,700	1,297,300	6,908,000

*Nassau population figures are included with Queens County up to 1900.

Later in the century and in the 1900's, most of the immigrants came from southern and eastern Europe, from Italy, Poland, Russia, Greece, Rumania and other countries in that part of the world. The Italians and the Poles, especially, were farmers in the old country, and so many of them sought jobs on the truck farms of Long Island. In World War I, many Negroes came to the New York area from Central America and the West Indies. An even greater number moved north from the southern states, seeking better opportunities. Although, at first, many settled in New York City, they later moved out on the Island. They were followed by many more, especially from 1930 on, as our nation became more mobile and industry grew on Long Island. The last important group to arrive has been the Puerto Ricans, our fellow citizens from the Caribbean Sea.

Today, Americans living on Long Island come from many stocks—English, Dutch, French, German, Negro, Spanish, Polish, Italian, Greek, Russian, Irish, Czech, Rumanian, Indian and others, all of whom have contributed to our community.

SUMMARY

The colonists became angry with the British government because they believed the British took away their rights. They objected to British restrictions on trade and British taxes. The Revolutionary War broke out when the Second Continental Congress declared independence on July 4, 1776. The people on Long Island were divided; some supported the British and others rallied round the Patriots. Long Island, itself, became a battleground. The British landed troops in Brooklyn and overran the American fortifications there in the Battle of Long Island. Then for seven long years Long Island was occupied by the British. Long Island became an important source of food and wood for the invaders. At times Patriots from Connecticut raided Long Island in whale boats and a spy ring operated here. Otherwise, the territory remained in British hands until the Treaty of Paris was signed in 1783 making America an independent country. Following the Revolution Long Island grew rapidly. It has become a land of many different peoples.

WHAT WORDS ARE MISSING?

The American colonists objected to British restrictions on (1). They also complained about paying (2) that the British laid upon them. The name of the Long Islander who signed the Declaration of Independence is (3).

Any American who sided with the British during the Revolution was called (4). Those who supported the rebels were known as (5). The most important fight on Long Island during the Revolution took place at (6). In Wallabout Bay many Americans died on (7). The British occupied Long Island during the Revolution for (8) years. During this time fighting continued by means of (9). Also, Setauket became an important (10) center. The Revolutionary War ended with the signing of the Treaty of Paris in the year (11). This treaty made America a (12) country.

Two reasons why immigrants came to Long Island after the Revolution are (13) and (14). The first Negroes came to America not as immigrants but as (15).

CHAPTER THINKING

1. Everybody pays taxes to the government. If this is such common practice why did the colonists become so violent over British taxes?

2. Was a Tory a bad American? Explain your answer.

3. America has always been a haven for those who could not find happiness elsewhere. Explain how this is so in connection with Long Island.

ACTIVITIES

1. Draw a pictorial map of the Revolution on Long Island showing:

   (a) Battle of Long Island
   (b) Whaleboat raids
   (c) Spying
   (d) Prison ships

2. Pretend that you are a member of a Long Island family with others in your class living in 1776. Have a family debate in which some members support the British and others support the Patriots.

3. Write and act out a play about the spy ring that operated on Long Island during the Revolution.

4. Draw a bar graph showing the growth of population from 1790 to 1970 for your county or for Long Island as a whole. (Nassau County starts in 1900.)

CHAPTER 5

Transportation and Communication on Long Island

This chapter and the ones immediately following it are devoted to a study of how Long Islanders both in the past and during present times make a living. The occupations of a community, taken together, are known as its "economic life." Before beginning a study of economic life on Long Island, we would do well to learn the reasons for the prosperity found in our community.

An important reason for many of the present day occupations on Long Island is New York City. New York is one of the greatest cities of the western world. Its population numbers 7½ million. Hundreds of thousands of additional people swell this figure traveling to New York City to work or to do business or to shop. New York is the trading center of the world. It is the richest city, the cultural center and the clothing capital of the United States.

In order to keep going, New York needs many of the things which Long Island can send to it. Its vast population needs the farm products Long Islanders can grow, the poultry we can raise, and the fish we can catch. For those people who do not wish to live in city apartments, New York needs our land for homes. It needs our beaches, our golf course, our parks, our race tracks and our waterways for recreation.

The people living on Long Island need much which New York has to give. First of all, New York City offers us jobs—jobs either in Manhattan itself, or on the island working at tasks which are required by the city, or by the people who work in the city. Furthermore, New York City offers us a fine shopping center to buy products such as clothing, jewelry, furniture and appliances. We go to New York to enjoy its excellent museums, theatres and night clubs. There is much give and take between New York City and Long Island. This, you must remember, is the outstanding economic fact about our Island.

If a man wishes to make a prosperous living, he must first have available good transportation and communication. Without the necessary land routes or waterways, he has no way to exchange his products for the products of others. For example, the Long Island farmer could not make any money if he had no means of getting his vegetables to market. His crops would rot on the farm. One's standard of living, therefore, depends to a large extent upon the excellence of transportation and communication in his community. Long Island, as we shall see, is well equipped in this respect.

WATER TRAVEL

Except for an occasional Indian trail, the first Long Island settlers had no roads. For a long time the sea acted as their chief means of transportation and communication. Hence, they built their settlements as close to the water as possible. This was especially true of those hardy folk who lived on the eastern end of Long Island. They found themselves large dependent upon boats in order to get around.

ORIGINAL FULTON STREET FERRY

The numerous protected waterways along the Sound and the South Shore made water travel the easiest way to visit or trade with other communities. If a village happened to be located inland, as was Hempstead, the nearest port became its shipping center. Farmers from Hempstead drove their cattle to Near Rockaway (present day East Rockaway) where there was an inlet and a wharf. At these landings, cattle, sheep and other farm products were loaded on ships and sent to New York City. The boat landings became the crossroads of traffic, where news and gossip were exchanged and where one met old friends.

To this day coal and oil and other heavy freight are hauled down the Sound by barge to these little ports. Sand and gravel are taken out in the same manner.

Ferries have played an important part in our economic history. The first ferry connecting Long Island with the rest of New York was established under Dutch rule. It connected Brooklyn with New Amsterdam. If you wished to go to New Amsterdam from Long Island, you went to where the foot of Fulton Street, Brooklyn, is located today. There you blew on a conch shell horn that hung from a tree near the water. On hearing the sound, a Dutch farmer, who was also ferryman, would come out of the fields, collect your fare first, and then row you across the East River in a small boat.

This service was improved as time went on, and later a large sailboat which could load sheep, cattle, horses and carriages, in addition to passengers, was used. The sailboat was difficult to manage against the wind and the swift tides of the East River.

In bad weather ferry customers were forced to wait, perhaps for several days, before a crossing to New York could be made. Therefore, inns and hotels were established near the ferry landing to put these customers up for the night. Brooklyn Ferry developed into a little village.

As Long Island became more populated the number of ferries grew until there were many regularly scheduled ferry routes connecting it with the mainland. However, with the great bridge building era, starting with the opening of the Brooklyn Bridge in 1883, the ferry lost its importance as a connecting link with New York City.

The ferries that operate today are given below. Several of them run only during the summer time.

Port Jefferson-Bridgeport, Connecticut
Orient Point-New London, Connecticut
Bay Shore-Fire Island points
Brown Point-Fire Island points
Patchogue-Fire Island points
Shelter Island-Long Island points

ROADS

In the early days, road building was practically unknown. The pioneers simply followed the Indian footpaths. Through constant use by farmers driving sheep, hogs, cattle and ox carts over them, these paths were gradually widened to form rough roads.

The first real road built on Long Island was officially called the King's Highway. Most of the inhabitants preferred to call it the Ferry Road because it ran to the ferry in Brooklyn. It was built during the 1700's and ran through the middle of Brooklyn to Jamaica. Later, it was extended to the eastern part of the island. At that time, the island was under the rule of Great Britain and, as in England, each important public road was known as the King's Highway. This road in Brooklyn still bears its original name.

When the King's Highway was completed, people living on Long Island could travel and transport goods by land as well as by water. Newspapers and mail could be more easily distributed.

For the most part, those who traveled the roads in those days traveled on foot or on horseback. Only the very rich could afford carriages.

For a while, the Royal Mail Coach operated over the King's Highway, the sight of which was quite an exciting event to the people who lived in the small villages along the way. By 1772, a passenger coach service was established between Brooklyn Ferry and Sag Harbor, the enormous distance of 120 miles! It took three days to make the trip, with regular stops at Hempstead, Smithtown, and St. George's Manor. How long would this same trip take you today traveling by automobile?

In addition to government-built roads, turnpikes were built on Long Island. A turnpike is a road built by a private company for profit. The profit came from the tolls which were charged at the toll gates to the users of the roads.

The first turnpike on Long Island was begun in 1806. The Jamaica and Rockaway Turnpike, as this private road was called, connected Rockaway and Jamaica. It was used to a large extent by vacationers from New York City who, even in those early days, came to Long Island to enjoy its beaches. Jamaica soon became the great turnpike center of the island and roads ran out of this village in all directions. Jericho Turnpike and Hempstead Turnpike are two of these roads which still bear their old names though they are now public highways.

The general pattern of roads on Long Island was laid down in 1773. Plans were made at that time for three main roads throughout the length of Long Island. There was to be a North Country Road, a South Country Road and a Middle Country Road.

Our modern system of highways is built around these three main routes: Route 25A follows the North Shore from Long Island City almost to Riverhead; Route 25 and the Long Island Expressway run down the middle of the island from Queens to Riverhead and points east; in the south, the Southern State Parkway, Belt Parkway, Sunrise Highway, and Route 27 run along the shore from Brooklyn to Montauk Point.

SOUTHERN STATE PARKWAY

Today, Long Island has some of the best roads in New York State. You all know the numerous concrete six lane highways which thread the countryside. Our parkways are beautifully landscaped with lawns, shrubs and trees. Clever "clover leaf" entrances, bridges and underpasses which bypass intersecting

"CLOVER LEAF" ON SOUTHERN
STATE PARKWAY

AN 1837 NEWSPAPER ADVERTISEMENT

cted for by the Agent, warranted. By order of the
ustees.   THEODORE EAMES,
Brooklyn, April 14, 1837—2aw3m Secretary B. C. C.

ong Island Rail Road Company·

N and after the 1st of May, the Cars will run as
follows, viz:

ave Hicksville.	Leave Jama'ca.	Leave Brooklyn,
7 o'clock, A. M.	7¾ o'clock, A. M.	9 o'clock A. M.
1 " A. M.	11¼ " A. M.	1 " P. M.
3 " P. M.	3¾ " P. M.	5 " P. M.

On SUNDAYS the 11 and 1 o'clock trains will be
itted.
Passengers will be received and left at the following
ces, viz:—Westbury, Clowesville, Delancy Avenue,
ion Course, Wyckoff's Lane and Bedford.
☞ Tickets can be had at the various Ticket offices.
ssengers who take seats without them, will be charged
a third more.
Freight trains will leave Hicksville every week day at 8
M. and Brooklyn at 4 P. M.; and all Goods designed to
sent by them, must be seasonably placed in the charge
he Agents in the Freight Department; as the Company
reby declare that they will not be responsible for
safe delivery of any articles not in the custody of the
ents; the only conclusive evidence of which must be en-
e, by the agents on the Registers, or Way Bills of the
mpany.   April 24—2awtf

roads, and the omission of signal lights, make driving on these parkways easier than on town roads.

Good roads have brought prosperity and growth to Long Island. Farmers can now ship their vegetables and poultry quickly to New York City or to other parts of the island. Trucking companies can deliver goods from New York City to Long Island communities. The commuter who works in New York but lives in a suburb of Long Island can drive his automobile back and forth to work. Vacationers can drive to the eastern resorts.

THE LONG ISLAND RAILROAD

We have only one railroad on Long Island today—the Long Island Railroad. Its history and present condition make an interesting story full of exciting events, troublesome times and much publicity.

The railroad came to Long Island in the 1830's. On April 18, 1836, our first railroad, the ten-mile-long Brooklyn and Jamaica, was completed. In the meantime, another railroad, which later became the Long Island Railroad, was formed in 1834. Plans were also laid to run a line from Brooklyn to Greenport. This railroad reached its destination in 1844.

Strange as it may seem, the reason for building this railroad was not so much to service Long Island, but rather to connect New York City with Boston. At that time a railroad ran from Boston to Stonington, Connecticut, but went no farther because the difficult terrain and many rivers made it extremely expensive to build the track through the remaining section of Connecticut.

The men of the Long Island Railroad thought that it would be profitable to build a line out to Greenport on eastern Long Island. From this point passengers could take a ferry across the Sound to Stonington and then proceed to Boston by railroad. In this way, the journey to Boston could be made in less time than it took otherwise.

A train ride in those days was quite an adventure. The cars were painted a bright yellow, and at first they were pulled by wood-burning locomotives with a large smoke stack belching black smoke and hot sparks. The rise was noisy and jerky as the train sped along at the "tremendous" speed of ten miles an hour. Sometimes the train had to come to a sudden stop because the track up ahead had been torn up by some angry farmers who objected to the railroad disturbing the peace of their farms.

For a while the line did quite well. But in 1848, when a railroad was finally put through on the mainland from Stonington to New York City, the Long Island Railroad lost much of its business. The Long Island has had many ups and downs like this ever since it was first started. It was necessary to build side lines which could be used by the people living in other parts of the island in order to operate profitably.

EARLY TRAIN

Meanwhile, other independent railroads began to appear on Long Island—about thirty of them. Most of them had only short runs, from village to village, much like our modern buses. But there were three main lines known as the North Side Railroad, the South Side Railroad and the Long Island Central. Competition among these lines became so keen that none of them was making any money, so the lines began to combine. By 1882, all the lines of the Island were part of one system, the Long Island Railroad.

In 1900, the Pennsylvania Railroad bought the Long Island Railroad. Then a large terminal was built in New York City for use of both railroads—the Pennsylvania Railroad Station. This terminal is the end of the line for passengers who commute to Manhattan.

Although the railroad made profits in the 1920's and during World War II most of the time, right down until today, it has been in bad financial condition. Finally, in 1965, the Long Island Railroad became part of the Metropolitan Transportation Authority. This is a public agency run by the state of New York.

It controls bridges, tunnels, airports, bus routes, subways and railroads in and around New York City.

PRESENT LONG ISLAND RAILROAD TRAIN

Today, the Long Island Railroad is primarily a commuter's line. While it also carries freight and mail, its chief work is to carry people to and from work. It is one of the busiest railroads in the nation. Look at these figures and you will see why.

Miles of track: 322
Trains per day: 700
Average number of commuters per day: 230,000

Jamaica is the center through which all Long Island trains, except the Port Washington ones, pass. Trains coming from the North Shore, from the South Shore and from the middle of the island go through Jamaica. Most of them are electric trains that get their electricity from a third, elevated rail. Some, those coming from the extreme eastern part of Long Island, are pulled by diesel engines. These locomotives are not allowed to go into New York City and the passengers must change at Jamaica. About 600 trains a day pass through Jamaica. It is said that more trains go through Jamaica Station every day than through any other railroad station in the United States.

THE FAMOUS BROOKLYN BRIDGE CONNECTS BROOKLYN AND DOWNTOWN MANHATTAN
This was the first bridge across the East River. It was completed almost 100 years ago and has been in use ever since.

BRIDGES AND TUNNELS

We must not forget the bridges and the tunnels when we study transportation facilities on Long Island. After the highways and railroads were built, passengers and shippers became impatient with the delays they met in making the crossing by ferry to New York. Therefore, in the middle 1800's, a movement was started to construct a bridge from Brooklyn, by then a big city in itself, across the East River. As in many great new undertakings, there were those who thought the project impossible. It was not until 1867 that the bridge was started.

John A. Roebling, an engineer who had just finished building the Niagara Suspension Bridge, was commissioned to construct the Brooklyn Bridge.

VERRAZANO-NARROWS BRIDGE

The ferries which once played such an important role are gradually being replaced by bridges. This one, named for the Italian who discovered New York Bay in 1524, joins Long Island and Staten Island.

Tragedy attended the raising of the span right from the start, as Roebling was killed while directing a survey for the bridge site.

His son, Washington A. Roebling, took up where his father left off. He, too, became a casualty of the great bridge when he was crippled by the dread sickness known as the "bends." While inspecting the foundations of the bridge towers, he stayed under water in compressed air too long and collapsed. But from his sick bed, with the help of his wife, he directed the building of the bridge until its completion on May 24, 1883.

It was the engineering wonder of the world, the largest suspension bridge ever to have been erected up to that time. It measured 1595 feet in length, took sixteen years to build and cost $16,000,000. So important an event was the completion of the Brooklyn Bridge that Chester A. Arthur, President of the United States attended the opening.

It started a new era on Long Island and tied our island more tightly to New York City than ever before. With its completion, it was possible for the Long Island farmer to drive his produce to New York City without any long ferry delays.

Soon other bridges, and later tunnels, were built anchoring Long Island highways and railroads to the mainland. The list includes at present:

> Brooklyn Bridge — Brooklyn to Manhattan
> Williamsburg Bridge — Brooklyn to Manhattan
> Manhattan Bridge — Brooklyn to Manhattan
> Queensboro Bridge — Queens to Manhattan
> Throgs Neck Bridge — Queens to The Bronx
> Triborough Bridge — Queens to Manhattan and The Bronx
> Whitestone Bridge — Queens to The Bronx
> Verrazano Bridge — Brooklyn to Staten Island
> Hellgate Bridge (railroad) — Queens to The Bronx
> Mid-Town Tunnel — Queens to Manhattan
> Long Island Railroad Tunnel — Queens to Manhattan
> Brooklyn-Battery Tunnel — Brooklyn to Manhattan
> Several East River subway tunnels

Recently, another bridge has been proposed to connect eastern Long Island with Connecticut, across Long Island Sound. At present, a Suffolk County resident must drive fifty miles or more into Queens if he wants to go to Connecticut and points north and cross over on the bridges there. Those who favor such a bridge claim that, in addition to saving time and gasoline, the bridge would bring more business and more tourists to Long Island. Howevewr, there is strong opposition, also. Those who oppose a fifteen-mile bridge across the Sound say that it will bring too much traffic to the island and will upset wildlife in the area.

AVIATION

Long Island is the aviation capital of the world. With its numerous airports and thousands of planes, Long Island leads all other communities in the amount of air traffic in its skies. Much overseas traffic from the United States bound for Europe, Africa and South America starts from Long Island. The island airports are full every day with passenger planes going to, and coming from, all parts of the United States and Canada. A plane lands at La Guardia Field every three minutes. Many sports planes are owned by Long Islanders and several aviation clubs are situated here.

While in some respects the topography of our island may be considered dull when compared with the grandeur of the Rocky Mountains, it is well suited for aviation. The flatness of southern Long Island makes it easy to build airplane fields without the expense of a great deal of artificial leveling. Also, the approaches to these fields are ideal for landing airplanes. Since we are surrounded on all sides by water and since we have no high hills, pilots can land and take off easily with few dangerous obstacles obstructing the way. Then, too, Long Island is situated on the ocean side of New York City, which is the logical place for an airport for airplanes going to, and coming from, Europe.

The history of Long Island aviation begins with army experiments in 1906 and in a big way with Glenn Curtiss in 1909. After seeing the Wright brothers' invention, Curtiss began to experiment with airplanes on the Hempstead Plains. He flew what was then the astounding distance of 25 miles in something that looked like a big box kite. Later, during the first World War, Long Island became an important military center. Two aviation camps were established here, Hazelhurst Field and Mitchell Field. Military planes came to be a common sight to the people of Hempstead as the pilots practiced their various maneuvers. Today, these fields no longer exist. On Mitchell field there are now two colleges—Hofstra University and Nassau Community College—and the Nassau County Veterans Memorial Colisseum.

(Courtesy of Nassau County Historical Museum)

GLEN CURTIS FLIGHT

After the war, more airplane fields were built. Passenger and private air traffic became more popular. In 1920, the first Transcontinental Air Mail Route from New York to San Francisco was inaugurated on Long Island.

It was from Roosevelt Field that Charles A. Lindbergh made the first non-stop airplane flight to Paris in 1927. This courageous young man took off from

Roosevelt Field in a monoplane named the "Spirit of St. Louis" at 7:52 in the morning on May 20. He pointed his plane out over the vast Atlantic Ocean and people all over the world waited anxiously to hear from him. At last, 33 hours and 3600 miles later, a tired but happy Lindbergh landed at Le Bourget Airfield near Paris. The world went wild over this daring feat.

(Courtesy of Nassau County Historical Museum

CHARLES LINDBERGH AND THE "SPIRIT OF ST. LOUIS"

Other famous fliers who left from Roosevelt Field include Post and Gatty who flew around the world and Howard Huges who also flew around the world. Roosevelt Field is now the site of a shopping center and light industry.

Many commercial, military and private airfields cover Long Island today. The biggest of them, and one of the world's largest, is John F. Kennedy International Airport on Jamaica Bay. On the other side of Queens is La Guardia Airport. These two fields handle most of the commercial and passenger air traffic for New York City. There are two military airports left on Long Island: Floyd Bennett Naval Air Station in Brooklyn and the Suffolk County Air Force Base. Two fields that handle private planes are Flushing Airport in Queens and Zahn's Airport near Amityville. There are other airports, too, which you can find by studying a good automobile map.

A visit to a major airport such as La Guardia Airport is an interesting experience. This busy center of activity is an exciting place. You may see the huge, curved, general administration building, with its bustling corridors where all the major airlines have ticket offices. There you can buy an airplane ticket to any part of the nation. In front of this building rises a tall, lighthouse-like control tower, so tall that its view is not hampered. This tower contains the officials who direct the air traffic, just like a policeman directs automobile traffic, only using radio signals instead of whistles. Each pilot receives a signal telling him when he may land his plane or when he may take off. The administration building also houses a very beautiful restaurant.

The hangars are gigantic. The huge doors are opened by motors. Inside, the planes are serviced; that is, they are cleaned, checked for safety, and repaired. Sometimes a complete motor is taken out of the plane and another one put in.

AIRPLANES TAKE OFF FROM KENNEDY INTERNATIONAL AIRPORT ON LONG ISLAND FOR ALL PARTS OF THE WORLD

COMMUNICATION

Long Island has enjoyed the advances in communication which were made elsewhere, just as the rest of the world has shared in these benefits. Thus when superior means of sending letters, sending messages and printing newspapers were developed, and the telephone and telegraph were invented, Long Island got its share of these modern means of communication. But, in addition, certain outstanding developments in communication originated on our island and certain noteworthy avenues of communication exist here today.

Long Island is the birthplace of American wireless telegraphy. In 1901, a pioneer radio station was established in the town of Babylon by which people on shore could communicate with ships at sea. This radio station kept the ships informed of the weather conditions and received emergency calls for help. In 1904, a radio station was erected at Sayville to send messages to Europe.

Today, although most of Long Island receives radio and television programs directly from New York City, it also has its own facilities. Here are a few of them in Nassau and Suffolk counties:

Television stations: Channel 21, Garden City
                      Channel 67 (WSNL) Central Islip

Radio stations: WIOK, Hempstead
                 WGBB, Merrick
                 WGLI, Babylon
                 WRCN, Riverhead

Newspapers are a part of the communications network on Long Island. There are many local newspapers that come out once a week. They are called "weeklies." For example, the *Baldwin Citizen* which has a circulation of 6000 copies comes out every Thursday. It concentrates on the news of Baldwin—what is happening in the schools, local club news, the local athletic teams and Little League, a visiting Congressman, and special events that take place in the community.

Long Island also has one very large daily newspaper, *Newsday*. It was founded in 1940 and at present has its headquarters and printing plant in Melville, Suffolk County. Since 1940 *Newsday* has grown to become one of the most important newspapers in the United States. These 1978 figures will tell you why:

Daily circulation: 495,000
Sunday circulation: 519,000
Approximate number of pages per daily issue: 150
Number of employees: 2,200
Number of carrier boys and girls: 9,800
Comparative position: Third largest evening newspaper
                      in the country

Newsday says that three out of every five families in Nassau and Suffolk counties read this newspaper. It carries both international and national news as well as local items. It contains special articles on many different subjects: education, health, sports, food, government, entertainment, and many others. *Newsday* plays an important part in the knowledge and thinking of Long Islanders.

There is one inventor in the field of communication who was a Long Islander. Ottmar Merganthaler, a Brooklynite, invented a method of setting type for books and newspapers which made use of a typewriter-like machine for casting an entire line of metal type at a time. It worked much more rapidly than the old fashioned hand-setting method. With his machine, called the linotype, it was possible to get news printed and on the newstands within an hour after it happened.

SOME PROBLEMS

During recent times transportation has become a serious problem on Long Island. One problem is whether or not we should encourage personal

LINOTYPE MACHINE
The man operating a keyboard, something like a typewriter, casts a entire line of metal type ready to be u in printing.

NEWSDAY — MELVILLE, N.Y.

transportation or mass transportation. Americans like to have their own cars so that they can go anywhere they please at any time they want. Also, automobiles are very convenient for carrying packages. However, we find that there are now so many automobiles on Long Island that during the rush hours even the very best roads are choked with traffic. Indeed, so slowly does the traffic move at 5 P.M. on the Long Island Expressway that it has been called "the longest parking lot in the world." Besides, all those automobiles, trucks, and buses emit gases that pollute the atmosphere. Furthermore, as the world runs out of oil supplies the cost of gasoline keeps going up and up.

Some people argue that we must do everything in our power to develop mass transportation. The least that can be done is to get people to travel to work together in car pools, instead of riding singly. Or, buses should be used more frequently. They say that the Long Island Railroad should be used more often.

Others argue that thus far mass transportation facilities are not good enough and need great improvement. The buses don't run often enough and they don't take you where you want to go. As for the Long Island Railroad, they say, it is far too expensive and too often late. For example, on December 12, 1978, the newspaper *Newsday*, carried this unbelievable story about the troubles of the Long Island Railroad on a particularly bad day:

> A series of breakdowns delayed more than half the Long Island Rail Road's rush-hour trains yesterday morning, causing an estimated 65,000 commuters to be late to work.

> "It was an absolutely miserable rush-hour," concluded LIRR spokesman Dave A. Vieser in reporting that the morning rush of 76 of 133 rush-hour trains experienced delays ranging from six to 80 minutes. He said that the majority of

the delays were from 40 minutes to an hour. Three trains were canceled because of the problems. . . .

The foulup began at 6:55 A.M. when the 6:52 from Babylon was delayed for 20 minutes at its first stop, Lindenhurst, because of a defective traction motor. This caused 10 to 15 minute delays on the next trains on the Babylon branch. Eight other trains on the same line were held up for another 20 minutes, according to Vieser, when the tower operator at Freeport sent the wrong train into a storage yard, and then had to turn it around.

The next blockage occurred at 7:20 A.M., when the 6:59 Hempstead train stalled, because of dead batteries, over a main switching point at Queens Village. This blocked four Main Line tracks until 8 A.M., and caused extensive delays on trains from Port Jefferrson, Huntington, Ronkonkoma, Oyster Bay and Speonk.

At 8:22 A.M., a major switch failed for 15 minutes just west of Jamaica Station, causing additional delays on all trains through Jamaica. No sooner had that problem been corrected than the 7:06 from Huntington became disabled west of Jamaica with brake trouble. "It was like a one-two punch," Vieser said of the two Jamaica breakdowns.

In the meantime, 1,000 passengers on the 7:35 from Huntington experienced what one passenger called "the final insult." After sitting it out near Belmont Racetrace for 30 minutes, his train inched its way through Jamaica and then began to pick up speed. "We whizzed through the tunnel, and I could see the lights of the platform." he recalled. "Then the train came to a dead stop. We had to back up into the tunnel, and we came in again, ending up in the Amtrak part of the station."

Vieser explained that this train had been misrouted onto Track 13 by an Amtrak tower operator and had to be rerouted to Track 12. . . .

The evening delays began shortly after the 5:31 to Hicksville reached the Queens end of the East River tunnel. At this point, according to railroad spokesman Kevin Cantwell, a pneumatic hose on the train's first car broke, causing the car to ride too low on the tracks. In an effort to make the car ride higher, Cantwell said, the train crew decided to move all the passengers out of the first two cars, and planned to detach the two cars from the train at a switching tower before Jamaica.

They managed to jam 255 passengers into the cars behind, Cantwell said, then discovered that there were still 100 passengers that wouldn't fit. So the train proceeded, getting to Jamaica 59 minutes late, and was taken out of service. In all, 22 trains were delayed by the 5:31. . . .

The airports have been a problem, too. More and more people are flying and the Long Island airports are jammed with air traffic. Airplanes may circle over Long Island for a long time waiting for permission to land. The officials say that more and larger airports are needed. But no one wants to live next to an airport with its roaring, earth-shaking noise of large jets taking off and landing. For example, in 1977, the inhabitants who lived near Kennedy Airport protested the landing of the British-French Concorde jet airplane. This supersonic (faster than sound) jet made more noise than others. Long Islanders tried to stop the plane from landing at Kennedy through court orders and picketing. Hundreds of automobiles blocked the roads to the airport in protest. However, it did not work. The government decided to allow Concorde planes to use the airport.

SUMMARY

In our study of economic life on Long Island thus far, we have learned that there are ample transportation and communication facilities for the Long Islander to carry on his business. On the land there are the highways and the Long Island Railroad to bear Long Island traffic. On, over, and under the water there are the ferries, bridges and the tunnels. For the air we have commercial, private and military airfields. Also, radio was pioneered on Long Island and there are many radio stations here today.

WHAT WORDS ARE MISSING?

The occupations of a community taken together are known as its (1). The very first settlers on Long Island shipped their produce by (2). One type of freight carried by barge today is (3). Ferries are not as important today as they were years ago because we now have (4). One ferry route in operation at present is the (5) route.

The first important road built on Long Island was called the (6). A turnpike is (7). The turnpike center of Long Island was located at (8). Today, three important highways on Long Island are (9), (10), and (11).

In 1844, (12) was connected with (13) by railroad. The original purpose in building the Long Island Railroad was (14). 1833 is an important date in Long Island history because (15) was completed in that year.

The name of the man who began experiments with airplanes on Long Island is (16). A famous trans-Atlantic flier who is associated with Long Island is (17). One important commercial airfield on Long Island is (18). One military airfield on Long Island is (19). The largest newspaper on Long Island is (20).

CHAPTER THINKING

1. The people who manufacture goods, who do farming and who fish on Long Island have excellent means of getting their products to market. Explain how this is true.

2. If Long Island were situated in the middle of the Atlantic Ocean its prosperity would suffer considerably. Explain.

3. Let us say that the state government agrees to give $100 million to Long Island to improve transportation. For what do you think this money should be used, to improve highways, to improve buses, or to improve the Long Island Railroad? Explain.

4. Would you favor or be against the building of a bridge across Long Island Sound to connect eastern Long Island with Connecticut?

ACTIVITIES

1. Draw a railroad map of Long Island showing all lines and some of the principal stations.

2. Do some research on Charles Lindbergh's flight in 1927 from Roosevelt Field to Paris and write a story about it to read to your class.

3. Do one of the following and report to your class on your experiences:

    (a) Take a trip on a Long Island ferry.
    (b) Visit a Long Island airport.
    (c) Visit a Long Island radio or TV station.
    (d) Visit the newspaper, *Newsday*.

4. Have a class debate on whether or not a bridge should be built across Long Island Sound connecting Connecticut with eastern Long Island.

THE OLD MOTT HOUSE, COWNECK.
Probably built about 1715.

(Courtesy of Nassau County Historical Museum)

CHAPTER 6

Farming on Long Island

The first people who settled on Long Island were farmers. Those who settled Hempstead found a plain running east and west where, as they said, "There is neither stick nor stone, and it produces a very fine grass which makes exceedingly good hay which is no small benefit to the town that owns it." So they cut down the forests and tilled the soil. The Indians helped them, showing the colonists how to plant corn and to fertilize each plant with a dead fish.

CATTLE AND SHEEP RAISING

In the main, the first Long Island farmers grew crops that they themselves could eat, such as corn and wheat, or crops which they could feed to their cattle and other livestock, such as hay and oats. Flax was grown to make linsey-woolsey, a cloth made partly of linen and partly of wool. Tobacco was raised to supply a local market.

However, it was not long before the colonial farmer realized that Long Island was an excellent place for raising livestock for market. The Hempstead Plains formed a natural pasture land, some 60,000 acres in size. There was plenty of fine marsh grass on the fringes of Long Island, excellent cattle fodder which could be had for the cutting. As the years went by, New York City grew larger and larger and demanded more and more farm products. It was a simple thing for the Long Island farmer to drive his sheep, hogs or cattle down to one of the landings and ship them by boat to the city. He soon found cattle raising his most profitable source of income, and Long Island became the Texas of Colonial America.

Several unique practices developed in connection with the cattle and sheep raising industries. For example, different farmers would use the same common grazing grounds for their cattle. Common grazing grounds were established on the Hempstead Plains, Cow Neck (now called Manhasset Neck), Rockaway Peninsula and Montauk Point.

Wherever it was possible, a fence was built across the neck of a peninsula and there sheep or cattle were allowed to graze all summer. For instance, Cow Neck was enclosed by a fence three miles long from water to water, consisting of 526 gates of fencing. Then, the right to pasture cattle on Cow Neck was divided among the sixty men who helped build the fence, in proportion to the number of gates each colonist constructed. These "gates rights" were precious and could be bought, sold or leased. At the town meetings one often heard complaints against individuals who failed to keep their part of the fence in good repair, or who forgot to close the gate, thus allowing the livestock to escape.

Once every year all the livestock would be driven to a large pen and there a "sheep parting," as it was called, took place. As each sheep or head of cattle was driven by, its owner would claim it on the basis of identifying ear marks. These ear marks were very carefully clipped. Each livestock raiser had his particular mark recorded in the town book, so that there would be no mistake in identifying his own property. The ear marks were handed down from father to son, or sometimes sold to another family.

"Sheep Parting Day" became a great holiday. With all the farmers and their families present for the sheep-parting, it became a time for contests such as foot racing, wrestling and horse racing. Merchants came to sell their wares. Tumblers, clowns and magicians came to entertain. A merry time was had by all—except, perhaps, by the poor sheep.

THE REVOLUTION

During the Revolution, Long Island was one of the chief sources of supply for the British Army. The British were well aware of the importance of Long Island as a farming community, as shown by General Howe's statement that this is "the only spot in America for carrying on the war with efficiency against the rebels. In this fertile island the army could subsist without any additional food supplies from England or Ireland. It has a plain on it, twenty-five miles long which has a fertile country around it. Forming their camp on the above plain, they could in five or six days invade and reduce any of the colonies at pleasure." So Long Island farmers were forced to sell, or give, to the British thousands of their cattle, sheep, poultry and swine. They were ordered to cut down their trees to supply firewood to their conquerors. Their grain fed the enemy soldiers. And if they refused to do so, their farms were destroyed and their cattle driven away.

WHEAT FARMING

With the Treaty of Paris ending the Revolutionary War in 1783, Americans began the work of mending their damaged farms. Land values rose rapidly. With the continued growth of New York City, the demand for farm produce increased. The Hempstead Plains became too valuable for mere pasture land, and the Long Island farmer turned to growing more wheat. The land was cultivated carefully, and soon Long Island became the "bread basket" of New York City.

(Courtesy of Nassau County Historical Museum)

CUTTING SALT HAY

On Eastern Long Island they built windmills to grind the grain into flour. Some of these huge four-armed giants stand today at places like East Hampton, Water Mill and Gardiners Island: They are English in origin, not Dutch, with eight sides, topped with a rotating cap to catch the direction of the wind. The arms might measure sixty feet.

The miller was an important person in the community. His place was a beehive of activity during the harvest season. His fee was usually one eighth of the wheat, which he took before grinding.

MARSHING

Marshing was another activity in which Long Island farmers engaged from early times until long after the Revolution. Along the South Shore are great stretches of marsh land on which grows a salt grass. It is fine feed for cattle. The people decided to give it a chance to grow before cutting it down. Therefore, no one was permitted to mow the grass before "Cutting Day" which was declared to be the second Tuesday in September.

The day before Cutting Day each farmer went to the marsh meadows to stake out his claim. He planned to camp there for a week and have a good time in the bargain. The next morning he went marshing, that is, cutting the salt grass. Each competed with the others to cut the most grass, because marsh grass was valuable and brought a good price on the market. Then it was loaded on boats and shipped to its destination.

Today, Long Island farming is somewhat different. Wheat is no longer a chief crop. Now the great wheat producing states of the Midwest supply us with most of our grains. Cattle and sheep have all but disappeared on Long Island since the Southwest and West supply us with meat. Long Island has, instead, turned to more profitable farming such as vegetables, potatoes, ducks, nursery stock and sod. At present, most farms are located in Suffolk County which, in terms of the economic value of the products, is the leading agricultural county in New York State.

GARDEN CROPS

On Long Island most farming is done on small farms. Our mild climate, which brings an early spring and keeps a late autumn, and our ample rainfall make Long Island an excellent place to grow garden crops. The soil and the land are well suited for this occupation, too, since there is no bedrock near the surface and in most places the land is level. This makes it possible to make the best use of farm machinery. Rapid means of transportation make delivery to the big city markets only a matter of hours.

The farms on Long Island produce crops valued in the tens of millions of dollars. These farms are worked intensively; that is, the farmer tries to get as much out of an acre of land as possible. With careful cultivation and the use of large quantities of fertilizer, the Long Island farmer earns a good return for his work and money.

FARM TRACTOR

(Courtesy of Rex Lyons)

The eastern end of the Island has become a district for growing such garden crops as strawberries, asparagus, Brussel sprouts, cucumbers and cauliflower. One of the interesting sights to see on Long Island occurs at strawberry time, in June. Because of the shortage of workers most strawberry farmers allow people to go into the fields to pick their own strawberries and pay for them by the basket. It's not unusual to see hundreds of people picking their own strawberries during harvest time. Long Island cauliflower, one of our leading crops, is well known and sold throughout the eastern United States. When the cauliflower ripens it is sent to Riverhead and Southold where it is auctioned off to the highest bidder. Other garden vegetables grown in large quantities are green beans, cabbage, spinach, sweet corn, lettuce and tomatoes. Some of these are grown during the winter in greenhouses. While it is expensive to grow vegetables in winter, they are sold quickly and profitably.

POTATO FARMING

Our most famous agricultural product is the potato. The potato is a tuber (root) which was first introduced to the European by the Indians of Mexico and Peru when Cortez and Pizarro conquered those countries. The Kahtadin potato used for cooking rather than for baking is the type of potato usually grown on Long Island.

Planting usually starts in the middle of March and continues through June. In this way the farmer has different fields of potatoes ready for harvest at different times. The farmer plants with seed potatoes which come principally from the state of Maine. A potato "seed" is actually a potato which has been cut into sections according to the number of "eyes" in it. From each eye a new potato plant will grow.

Throughout the growing season, the farmer exercises much care in cultivating the potato. From two thousand to three thousand pounds of fertilizer will be used per acre. He does most of his work with costly machinery. There is a four row planter, which plants the potatoes. He has weeders, sprayers, dusters and perhaps he may hire an airplane to spray or dust his plants in order to keep his crops in a healthy state.

Harvest time starts in August and continues until October. The potato farmer harvests his crop with a machine which digs up the potatoes and may collect or leave them ready to be collected. The crop is then graded by a machine into Number One and Number Two potatoes, the Number Two being the smaller. Next, the potatoes are packed into one-hundred-pound bags and shipped by motor truck to the farmers' markets in New York City.

About 27,000 acres of farmland are devoted to growing potatoes in Suffolk County which is one of the largest potato producing counties in the United States. Through careful cultivation our farms produce an average yield of 250 hundred-pound bags of potatoes per acre—one of the highest in the country. King Potato rules the Long Island farmland. Once a year, at Riverhead, a Potato and Vegetable Harvest is held, at which time a pretty girl is crowned as his Queen.

POTATOES BEING HARVESTED ON A LONG ISLAND FARM
On most of the larger farms, machines are used for harvesting potatoes but, on some smaller farms, the potatoes are dug up by hand and placed in baskets for grading.

DUCK FARMING

The Long Island duckling holds the number two spot among our most famous farm products. Moriches Bay and Riverhead are the duck regions. Along the creeks which run into the Bay may be seen hundreds of thousands of white ducks. The breed is the white Pekin, a duck introduced to this country from China in the 1870's. It is a large meaty bird served as a delicacy in the best restaurants.

Duck raising is big business on Long Island. There are only about 27 real duck farms, but each farm raises from 40,000 to 600,000 ducks apiece each year. From five to seven million ducks, or fifty percent of the United States' total are raised on Long Island each year.

THREE OUT OF EVERY FIVE DUCKS IN THE UNITED STATES ARE RAISED ON LONG ISLAND FARMS
Many thousands of ducks are raised on this Certified Dux Farm at East Moriches and on other
similar farms in Suffolk County.

The duckling starts his short life in an incubator. Here he is hatched along with thousands of his brothers and sisters. From the incubator the duckling moves to the brooder where it stays until six weeks of age. It then graduates to the water front to be fattened for market. When the duck is from five to six pounds, it is slaughtered. This is done in a large processing plant in Eastport. The feathers are plucked and sold as a by-product to make pillows and mattresses. The duck itself is packed in an ice barrel or quick-frozen.

Other poultry products raised on Long Island include chickens, turkeys, geese and eggs.

NURSERIES

Long Islanders appreciate plants which lend beauty to their environment as
well as plants which can be eaten. Flowers, shrubs, trees and evergreens for
landscaping purposes are grown in large quantities. This is the nursery industry, more scientifically known as *horticulture*.

Our Dutch ancestors started us in this business when they brought their tulip
bulbs with them from Holland to brighten up their gardens in America. Then
the Prince family, of French Huguenot descent, established a nursery at
Flushing which became world famous.

AT THIS LONG ISLAND NURSERY THOUSANDS OF FLOWERING PLANTS ARE GROWN IN GLASS HOUSES

William Prince, who lived during the Revolution, made this nursery the marvel
of the age. He imported plants from every corner of the globe, from Europe,
Japan, China, Australia, and other far-off places. Many noted men of his time,
among them George Washington, visited it. Today Flushing is known for its
beautiful trees. It is believed that 2,000 varieties from all over the world grew
there.

The demand for the produce of our modern nurseries has become increasingly
greater as more and more homes are built on Long Island. These homes are

surrounded by trees, shrubs and flowers which come from nurseries. A great nursery area exists between Brookhaven and Sayville where there are acres and acres of glass roofed hot houses. There is a famous nursery at Westbury, founded by Isaac Hicks in 1852. These nurseries grow many kinds of shrubs, shade trees, evergreens and ornamental trees. Flowers are grown in greenhouses and include varieties such as chrysanthemums (mums, for short), poinsettias, azaleas and geraniums. About $30 million in flowers are grown each year. The nursery and flower growing industries are profitable on Long Island.

AT THE NEW YORK STATE AGRICULTURAL COLLEGE AT FARMINGDALE STUDENTS LEARN TO BE FARMERS

OTHER FARMING

Long Island farmers engage in other farm activities on a smaller scale. There is some dairy farming in Nassau and Suffolk counties to supply the local market with milk, butter and cream. There are cranberry bogs in the swamps along the Peconic River. Wheat growing is occasionally practiced and many farmers have some fruit trees, especially apple trees for making apple cider in the fall.

Lastly, there is sod, or grass growing. About 3,000 acres of Suffolk's farmland is used for growing grass that is sold to make "instant lawns." The sod farms are located mostly in Brookhaven and Riverhead. They are huge, flat green carpets. After the grass is grown it is harvested with a special machine called a sod harvester. A knife cuts the sod from the soil. Each strip is about 15 inches wide and is cut in 4 to 6 foot lengths. Very little soil is removed with the sod, usually not over a half-inch. The strips of sod are folded and loaded on pallets, mechanically, and hoisted on trucks to be delivered to homes, commercial buildings, athletic fields and highway shoulders.

THE STATE UNIVERSITY AGRICULTURAL AND TECHNICAL INSTITUTE

At Farmingdale, the state government maintains a college where young people can learn to be good farmers, experts on agriculture, or specialists in other fields. Some students are taught the latest practices in scientific farming during class time and then are given a chance to try them out on the many acres of farm land and the hundreds of livestock which the Institute owns. A graduate from this course is more certain of becoming a successful farmer.

SOME PROBLEMS

Life is not easy for Long Island farmers. They face a number of difficult problems. For one thing crops and livestock are constantly being attacked by pests or diseases. In the case of the potato it is the Golden Nematode, which is a tiny worm, that attacks the plant root. Also, if the farmer does not keep careful watch the European corn borer will chew its way through his corn crop. Ducks get diseases such as Duck Cholera and Duck Plague and have to be destroyed. People also complain that the duck farms have an awful smell and they pollute the bays and streams.

Some of these troubles are being corrected by scientific research. For example, there is a Long Island Duck Research Laboratory at Eastport. Vaccines and plant sprays have been developed to help the farmer overcome his problems.

SUMMARY

The first occupation on Long Island was farming. It still is an important occupation. First, cattle raising and then wheat growing were the chief farm activities. Today, Long Island farmers engage principally in the raising of garden crops, potatoes, ducks, and ornamental plants. Farming is a profitable business on Long Island.

WHAT WORDS ARE MISSING?

The first important farm occupation on Long Island was the raising of (1). "Sheep parting" refers to (2). After the Revolution the most important crop on Long Island was (3). During the marshing season in the early 1800's Long Island farmers (4). Today, our most famous Long Island agricultural product is (5). The second most important farm product is (6). A farm that grows shrubs and trees is called (7). A general name for farm products such as string beans, cucumbers, cauliflower and tomatoes is (8). Grass that is grown to be sold in strips for lawns is called (9). The name of the college on Long Island that is devoted to the improvement of farming is (10).

CHAPTER THINKING

1. Would you like to be a farmer? Why? Why not?

2. Do you see the possibility of sod farms having a bad effect on the environment? Explain your answer.

3. Do you think Long Island will be an important farming area of New York State by the year 2000? Explain.

ACTIVITIES

1. Select one of the farm products mentioned in this chapter, get more information about it and report to your class.

2. Make a picture booklet of Long Island farm products with appropriate explanations.

3. Visit a farm and interview the farmer about his product and his methods. Report to your class.

CHAPTER 7

Fishing, Yesterday and Today

Fishing comes naturally to Long Islanders. Whether for pleasure or for profit, ever since the first white man set foot on this shore, fishing has played an important role in our history. The mere fact that we live on an island encourages us to reap the harvest of the sea. The island is indented with numerous bays and inlets where billions of fish seek shelter from the ocean in order to spawn (give birth). These are ideal fishing grounds. The early inhabitants of Long Island, particularly those on the east end, became fishermen as well as farmers in order to add sea food to their diet.

WHALING

The first fishermen knew all the fish which we catch today. Furthermore, they engaged in a very exciting catch which has now become all but extinct in Long Island waters—whales!

In the 1600's and 1700's, whales were not an uncommon sight off the coast of Long Island. Occasionally one of them would be washed up on the beaches off East Hampton or Southampton. One day in the year 1700 a woman, who happened to be traveling between East Hampton and Bridgehampton, counted thirteen whales stranded on the beach.

At that time whales were valuable for whale oil which was used to light lamps and for the flexible bone used to make corsets and umbrellas. It brought a high price on the market. As the demand for whale oil, and the flexible whale bone, grew, townspeople set up a "whale watch." The watcher was stationed on top of some high sand dune. When the tell-tale black hulk and white spume of a whale rose out of the water, it was the duty of this person to arouse the town with the cry of "Whale off!"

Quickly the farmers would drop their plows and take to the little whaleboats which stood ready on the shore for this purpose. They attacked the whale with crude harpoons as the Indians had taught them. The whale was brought onto the beach. The blubber was peeled off in big chunks and thrown into try pots to boil out the oil.

Long Islanders did not have the whale business all to themselves. By the 1800's they found that competition from other places on the mainland and other islands, was driving them out of the whaling business. The whalers of Nantucket, in particular, were beating them to the whales. The whales coming down from the north, passed Nantucket before showing off the Long Island coast. Naturally, Nantucketers had first chance at them and they took good advantage of this.

It was not long before our people set out in large ships to go hunting for the whales, wherever they might be, instead of waiting until they appeared off our shores. With this new development, the center of whaling activity shifted from the South Shore to the quiet and deep waters of Peconic Bay, or to Long Island Sound, which could better shelter large vessels.

Sag Harbor became a thriving center for whaling. At least fifty large whaling vessels considered this town their home port. Some of its whaling ships were away for three years at a time, hunting down the giant mammals* of the deep. They visited such far off places as the Pacific Ocean and the Antarctic.

It took a great amount of preparation to make these trips. Coopers made barrels to hold the oil; blacksmiths fashioned whaling tools; sail makers repaired the canvas. There were whaleboat builders, provisioning men, and countless other people supplying the whaling industry. For some time after the Revolution, Sag Harbor was considered nearly as important a port as New York City itself.

THIS WHALE CAME TOO NEAR HUNTINGTON AND WAS STRANDED WHEN THE TIDE WENT OUT
Whales sometimes grow to be 100 feet long. Before petroleum was discovered in Pennsylvania in 1859, whale oil was much in demand for home lighting and for industrial purposes.

* A whale is not a fish; it is a mammal or warmblooded animal related to those you find on land.

LARGE, SQUARE-RIGGED SAILING VESSELS SAILED OUT FROM SAG HARBOR IN SEARCH OF WHALES
These ships sometimes sailed far south into the Antarctic Ocean and were gone for a year or two until they had obtained a full cargo of whale oil which could be sold at a good price.

John Fordham, a blacksmith who lived during those times described Sag Harbor at the height of its whaling days during the 1840's.

I remember when black, bull-bowed whale ships lay three abreast along yonder dock, and eight hundred coopers, riggers, sailmakers and stevedores went to and from the wharves to their work in the morning and evening. In cellars along shore thousands of barrels of oil lay piled tier on tier and covered with sea weed. Yonder were great warehouses, three stories high, their upper stories filled with spermaceti and whalebone, the lower used as sail lofts and rigging lofts, and cheek by jowl with them were long cooper shops and here and there a . . . candle factory. The bosom of the bay was covered with lighters, piled high with products of the whale coming from ships at anchor and returning with provisions and outfits. An army of carts were moving oil and bone from the docks, the cooper's adse and the blacksmith's hammer made merry music all day long, and the streets were filled with crews of incoming and outgoing vessels, attended by their wives, daughters, sisters or sweethearts, making a strange jumble of welcome and farewell, smiles and tears, weeping and laughter.

Captains, mates and crew all sailed on the lay — that is, for a certain share of the cargo secured. This percentage varied with the different merchants and captains, but as a rule the captain received one-sixteenth, the mate one-twenty-fourth, the boat steerer one-sixtieth, and ordinary seamen one-onehundred and tenth. The remainder belonged to the owners, who for their part furnished the ship and bore all the expense of the outfitting. . . .

It was no light job to fit out a whale ship . . . in the forties. First the sails, rigging and boats were inspected with the greatest of care, for on those depended the safety of the vessel and the crew, and of course her success. . . .

This done the captain picked out his crew of twenty-two men, aiming to get the most expert at his command, and ranging the country from Montauk to Shinnecock for them. The crew was a motley lot when gathered — whites, Indians, half-breeds, negroes — but they were picked men.

To complete the outfit there was to be provided three boats, with tubs, harpoons, lances lines, hatchets, spades, etc., with from two to three thousand barrels well seasoned and a great variety of provisions and miscellaneous stores.

A whalers homecoming from a three year's voyage was an event. As soon as she was sighted down the bay a pilot boat would put off with the owners and friends of the whaler's officers on board to meet and welcome her. Meantime the news would spread through the village, and as soon as the vessel drew up to the dock the latter was often black with friends and neighbors of the crew gathered to welcome them. It was not always rejoicing, though, for often the story told in the log book of some fine fellow in his youth crushed in the whale's jaw, or dying of fever on board.

While whaling was a dangerous business which took sailors to distant places for a long period of time, men were willing to take the risks and hardships because of the rich reward. Some voyages netted as much as $75,000 a ship, which was a great sum of money in those days. However, with the discovery of petroleum in the middle 1800's, whale oil lost its first place as a fuel for lamps.

Gradually the whaling industry declined. The last whaling ship sailed out of Sag Harbor in 1871, and the once busy port became a quiet little town. Today, if you should go to Sag Harbor, you will see there a whaling museum to remind you of the former glory of this little village.

MENHADEN FISHING

Menhaden fishing is another industry carried on in early days which we do not practice to any great extent today. Menhaden is the Indian word for fertilizer, and the menhaden fish were used to fertilize the farmer's crops. Hundreds of millions of fish come to spawn in the protected waters of the Great South Bay. Among them are the mossbunder and several other varieties which are not good to eat. Long Island farmers were taught by the Indians how to make use of these fishes by spreading them on fields to rot into the soil, thus enriching it.

As other and better chemical fertilizers came into use, menhaden fish continued to be caught for different reasons. It was found that the oil of the fish

1. OYSTER BOATS START OUT FROM GREENPORT

2. A DREDGE SCOOPS UP THE OYSTERS

3. THE METAL WIRE BASKET FILLED WITH OYSTERS IS EMPTIED ON THE DECK. THE OYSTERS ARE SHOVELED INTO A PILE UNTIL THE DECK IS FULL

4. BACK AT THE DOCK OF THE BLUEPOINT COMPANY, THE BOAT UNLOADS THE OYSTERS ONTO A CONVEYOR WHERE THEY ARE CARRIED TO THE FACTORY

OYSTERS ARE OPENED BY HAND

Oysters are sold in two different ways: 1, by the barrel in their original shells, or 2, in cans after being opened and graded according to size.

Below, we see oysters being canned after having been graded and washed in the processing plant of the Bluepoint Company

could be used in paints and for tanning, as a substitute for more expensive oils. Factories were built along the South Shore to boil the oil out of the fish. However, the offensive odors from these fish factories were so objectionable that the people of the community forced the factory owners to move their establishments to isolated, uninhabited places. Today, menhaden fish are no longer processed on Long Island. Menhaden fishermen take their catch to fish factories located in other states.

SHELLFISH

As Long Island's farmlands have long been known for potatoes, its fisheries have been famous for oysters. Indians and early white men fully realized the value of this shellfish as a food, and oysters were highly prized among them. Moreover, oysters became big business when a huge bed of these shellfish was discovered off Blue Point in the Great South Bay about one hundred-twenty years ago.

The Blue Point oyster achieved a worldwide fame. There, protected from the ocean and breeding in the quiet waters of the bay, oysters were to be found by the millions. They were of a very high quality, fat and mild, as a result of the mineral content of the coastal waters of this area. The Blue Point quickly became so popular that in order to prevent other localities from selling their oysters as "Blue Points," it was necessary to restrict by state law the name to mean only those oysters raised in the Great South Bay.

Modern oyster fishing is really oyster farming. The oysterman raises oysters to-day in much the same way as the farmer raises his crops, except that the oyster farms are under water. They are planted by the acre just as crops are planted by the acre. The grounds are leased by large oyster companies from the nearby towns.

The Long Island oysterman gets most of his oyster "seed," that is, tiny baby oysters, from Chesapeake Bay or Connecticut. The tiny oyster seeds are laid on a bed of old oyster shells to which they attach themselves. When they attain a certain size the oyster seeds are raked up and transplanted to shell-growing waters in Gardiners Bay or other Long Island oyster grounds. Later, they are transplanted to a depth of from 12 to 18 feet.

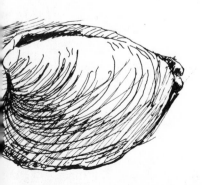

It takes about five or six years for the oyster to grow to a size ready for market. During this time, the oyster farmer must keep the oyster bed clean and protected from starfish and drills which are deadly enemies of the oyster. When the oysters are large enough, they are dredged up from their comfortable beds by the baymen and sent to one of the oyster packing houses located around Greenport.

There are many other shellfish caught off the coast of Long Island, including clams, scallops, lobsters and crabs. Long Island markets more clams than any part of the country. In 1977, 55 percent of the hard shell clams sold in the

United States came from Long Island. Most of them were raked up from the shallow, sandy bottom of the Great South Bay. Indeed, so important an occupation is clamming on the island that the nickname for an old-time Long Islander is "Clamdigger." In comparison with the oyster industry which is carried on by large companies, the clamdigger works by himself, for himself, in small boats.

FIN FISH

Another class of fish caught in Long Island waters is the fin fish—those fish that swim in the ocean by means of fins. It is a large industry carried on by fishermen who fish in both the Atlantic Ocean and the Long Island bays. Although the Federal Government passed a law in 1976 extending the U.S. controlled fisheries to 200 miles off our coast, Long Island commercial fishermen usually stick close to the land.

The most important fishing towns where most fish landings (bringing in the fish) are made are Montauk, Greenport, and Freeport. Here, fishing boats land their catches every day to be shipped off immediately to New York City or local markets. These ports are good places to buy fresh fish. For example, many people go to the Freeport docks to purchase fish a few minutes after it comes off the boat.

A good number of Long Islanders make their living from fishing. In 1975 there were approximately 3,000 full-time and 6,000 part-time commercial fishermen in Nassau and Suffolk counties. Also, hundreds of others were engaged in related jobs such as fish-packing, transportation and fish-processing.

Long Island waters abound with a great variety of fin fish. When we think about how valuable the catch is, flounders lead the list. In 1977, Long Island commercial fishermen caught $1½ million worth of flounders. Other fin fish caught in large quantities include porgies (scup), bluefish, Atlantic mackerel, sea trout, striped bass, butter fish, and whiting. That does not end the list. There are dozens of varieties caught in smaller quantities such as sea bass, eels and sharks. There is no lack of fish, either in the quiet bays or in the ocean on the "outside." Following is a table showing the 1977 landings on Long Island.

	Nassau	Suffolk	Total
Fin Fish — Pounds	771,000	17,299,000	18,070,000
Fin Fish — Value in dollars	274,000	5,534,000	5.808,000
Shell Fish — Pounds	3,778,000	15,408,000	19,187,000
Shell Fish — Value in dollars	2,216,000	24,944,000	27,160,000
Total Fish — Pounds	4,549,000	32,409,000	36,958,000
Total Fish — Value in dollars	2,490,000	30,478,000	32,968,000

(Courtesy of Rex Lyons)

FISHERMEN HAULING IN CATCH

LARGE "GILL NETS" MUST BE KEPT IN CONSTANT REPAIR

Have you ever noticed a long row of stakes sticking out of the water just off shore? Those are fish traps set by fishermen to catch the harvest of the sea. On these poles, are strung fish nets creating a "wall" to guide the fish into a huge pocket net from 50 to 75 feet in diameter. It is almost impossible for them to escape.

Fish are also caught with "gill nets," nets which are designed to catch the fish by entangling their gills. The net is allowed to hang down in the water from a series of cork floats, stretched out in a long line. The fishermen frighten schools of passing fish into the net or surround the fish with the long net. Then the net is hauled in and the fish are taken off.

Long Island fishermen are independents, not company men. Most of them own their own boats and operate on a small scale. They must know the tides, the currents, and the winds favorable for fishing. They must know the sea bottom and the habits of the fish. Above all, they must be good sailors.

FISHING FOR FUN

Whether you fish with a dangling string from a dock, or outfit yourself with an expensive rod and reel and board a party boat headed into the ocean, one of the keenest sports on Long Island is fishing. About 36 percent of all fish caught off Long Island is landed by sports fishermen. Furthermore, it is surprising to learn that sports fishermen catch more of certain kinds of fish than do commercial fishermen who make a living from it. This is especially true for striped bass and blue fish.

Generally speaking there are three kinds of sport fishing: surf fishing, fishing from piers and similar places, and boat fishing. The surf angler may be seen along any of our beaches, casting his line into the breakers and slowly reeling it in. He is after striped bass, prize catch of the surf angler. But bluefish, weakfish and channel bass are also popular with him.

The boat angler may find anything—flounder, bluefish or weakfish—if he is in the bay. He can also hire a charter boat, one which is large enough to accommodate a small group of people, and withstand the rough ocean waters in order to track down the torpedo of the sea, the tuna. Imagine the thrill of catching a 300- or 400-pound tuna!

For those anglers who like the pull of fresh water trout on their line, there are several streams and lakes on Long Island stocked with this fish. The state maintains a fish hatchery at Cold Spring Harbor where brown trout are raised by the thousands. When they reach a certain size, they are loaded into a tank truck and then dumped into fresh-water streams and lakes such as those found at Belmont Lake State Park.

(Courtesy of Rex Lyons)

FISHING TRAWLER

GIANT TUNA FISH LIKE THIS ONE ARE CAUGHT IN LONG ISLAND WATERS
These game fish may weigh from 600 to nearly 1,000 pounds. It may take the fisherman with rod and reel several hours to land these fish which grow to ten feet in length.

SOME PROBLEMS

The quantity of fish caught in Long Island waters is going down, not up. For instance, in 1880, 150,000 metric tons of fish were landed. But in 1970, only 15,000 metric tons of fish were caught, or 10 percent of the firstt figure. The reasons for this drop include overfishing, pollution and natural causes.

The oyster industry is a good example of these problems. Because of overfishing it was not long before the natural oyster beds were exhausted by the "baymen," as the oyster fishermen are sometimes called. At first, the baymen fished in small rowboats with iron-toothed rakes or long pairs of tongs. But later, in order to supply the hungry New York markets, they took to fishing in large boats using dredges to scrape from the bottom of the bay as many oysters as possible. Also, the waters near the big villages became polluted with sewage and other wastes. Health authorities had to forbid the use of such polluted waters for oystering. Soon there were scarcely any marketable oysters left. So the state and many of the towns, in an attempt to save the oyster beds from complete extinction, passed regulations about oystering. The oystermen were required to lease underwater land from the towns. Sanitary methods of disposing sewage and garbage were adopted to keep the bays clean and the oysters uncontaminated.

There were other oyster troubles, too. The Great South Bay had lost its cleansing bath of Atlantic Ocean water when storms filled Moriches Inlet, and the oysters died of suffocation by the millions. On the north, Long Island Sound and its branches developed a plague of starfish, small animals that can open and eat oysters. The starfish were so numerous that one dredge reported taking up as many as 1,200 bushels a day. The oystermen carry on a continuing battle to overcome these problems.

SUMMARY

Long Island, which is shaped like a fish, is a natural place for fishing. Its protected bays have become the breeding grounds for countless millions of fish. Therefore, fishing has been an important occupation for a long time giving employment to thousands of people. The early settlers went after whales and menhaden fish as well as the fish we have today. At present there are many varieties of fish which are caught both commercially and for sport. Long Island is also noted for its shellfish.

WHAT WORDS ARE MISSING?

The calm waters of Long Island bays form a protected place in which fish may (1). An important center for whaling ships in early days was (2). Whale oil was used for (3). The whaling industry declined because of the discovery of (4). Menhaden fish were used by the Indians and early colonists for (5). One use of menhaden fish today is (6).

The name of a famous type of oyster on Long Island is (7). The center of the oyster industry on Long Island is (8). We do not say oyster fishing; we say oyster (9). Two other shellfish caught in Long Island waters are (10) and (11).

Five fin fish caught in Long Island waters are (12, 13, 14, 15 and 16). A fish weighing several hundred pounds which is a prize catch for sportsmen is the (17). One way in which commercial fishermen catch fin fish is with a (18). A state maintained hatchery is located at (19). This hatchery raised (20).

CHAPTER THINKING

1. Would you like to be a commercial fisherman? Why? Why not?

2. One of the problems our fishermen face today is the pollution of local waters. How would you handle this problem?

ACTIVITIES

1. Make a picture booklet of fish caught in Long Island waters.

2. Get some information about the whaling industry and report to your class. If possible visit the whaling museum at Sag Harbor.

3. Interview a fisherman and ask him questions about his work.

CHAPTER 8

Industry on Long Island

In addition to farming and fishing, Long Islanders also make their living from manufacturing. Indeed, Long Island, all four counties, is the fourth largest industrial section of the United States. The following figures show the importance of industry. Recently the approximate number of factories for the four counties was:

Kings	4,800
Queens	2,800
Nassau	2,400
Suffolk	1,600
Total	11,600

The approximate number of factory workers was:

Kings	146,500
Queens	108,600
Nassau	93,500
Suffolk	60,600
Total	409,000

We can see that a large number of Long Islanders depend upon factory work for their income. Can you also see, from these figures, that this is truer for western Long Island than it is for the eastern part?

Let us now briefly make an overview of the variety of products manufactured in each county. Then, let us examine a few key industries more deeply such as shipbuilding, the aerospace industry and our nuclear research laboratories.

MANUFACTURING IN BROOKLYN

It would take a long time to describe the many articles made in Brooklyn (Kings County) for there are over 700 industries. One reason for Brooklyn's importance in manufacturing is its location. Brooklyn sits on New York Bay, the chief point from which exports from the United States are sent to foreign countries. Also, this borough* of New York City is the center of a vast population extending eastward through Long Island and westward through Manhattan. The Brooklyn Chamber of Commerce says Brooklyn has the largest regional marketplace in the United States. Millions of people buy the goods Brooklyn produces.

Five major industries lead the rest. They are apparel, food, metals, machinery and electrical equipment. Also, Brooklyn is one of the world's centers for the roastinig of coffee beans. Following is a sample list of specific articles Brooklyn manufactures; a complete list would fill several pages:

rope	silk stockings
soap	mirrors
shoes	saxophones
beer	tooth paste
paint	airplane parts
candy	bed springs
spaghetti	bathroom scales
lead pencils	cod liver oil

MANUFACTURING IN QUEENS

Queens, too, is an important manufacturing area. Its factories hug the waterfront and the great railroad yard, the largest in the world, in Long Island City. Long Island City is the center of Queen's industries. Queens' factories specialize in food processing. Second in importance is apparel, and third is electrical machinery. Also, Steinway pianos, furniture, Bulova watches, and metal products are produced in Queens, to mention a few.

LONG ISLAND CITY IS THE HUB OF QUEENS' INDUSTRIES
In this freight yard in Long Island City we see a trainload of coal being brought into the Long Island City factories while other trains stand by to take the factory products to all parts of the nation.

MANUFACTURING IN NASSAU-SUFFOLK

The two suburban counties of Long Island, Nassau and Suffolk specialize in defense industries. In other words they manufacture military equipment for the United States Air Force and the Navy. In 1974, 57 percent of the factory workforce, 87,658 employees, was employed in making metals, machinery, electrical equipment, transportation equipment, and instruments for our armed forces. Because of this, Nassau-Suffolk industry depends greatly on government contracts.

However, in addition to the large military manufacturing plants, there are numerous small establishments that supply other products. Among them are clothing and textiles, chemicals, paper products, printing and publishing and rubber and plastic goods.

Nassau County also has a very fine place for people who want to work but are physically handicapped. It is the world's first and only national center on Employment of the Handicapped located at the Human Resources Center in Albertson. Here, despite their handicap, people are trained for jobs they are able to do. It's surprising how much work a handicapped person can do if he is encouraged.

SHIPBUILDING AND COMMERCE

Shipbuilding on Long Island dates back long before the Revolution. Our shipyards have turned out many proud vessels that have played an important part in the history of the nation.

(Courtesy of the Port Authority of N.Y. and N.J.)

PIER 6 IN BROOKLYN

There are several reasons why Long Island became a shipbuilding center. Our trade with New York City before the opening of good roads and the coming of the Long Island Railroad meant that most of our produce had to be carried by water. Small coastwise boats were needed for this. This helped establish the shipbuilding industry. Also, our fishermen needed boats, boats for the shallow waters of the bays, and boats to withstand the rough ocean. When whaling was in its prime, great ocean-going schooners were built on the island to track down the huge creatures.

Long Islanders were able to build ships because we were fortunate enough to have growing here good supplies of locust and oak trees, two varieties of timber used in shipbuilding. Furthermore, our irregular coast line offered many protected harbors in which to build shipyards. Lastly, the western end of Long Island, that part called Brooklyn, is situated along the excellent New York Harbor, to which ships come from all over the world. Many of these ships need repairs or refitting, and the Brooklyn shipyards handle much of this work.

Shipyards were also established around such sheltered places as Cold Spring Harbor, Stony Brook, Greenport and Port Jefferson. All kinds of sailing boats were constructed there, including fishing smacks, whaling ships, sloops, schooners, brigs, and barks. Port Jefferson in particular became an important shipbuilding community in the 1840's. Some of the famous China Clippers were built here. Slavers were built for the African trade, and this port became one of the points in the "triangular trade" to the West Indies and Africa.

With the coming of the Steel Age, wooden sailing vessels gave way to iron ships and steam. Long Island has no coal and iron nearby to compete with modern shipbuilding centers. Consequently, the day of building big ships has passed for us, with the occasional exception of the Brooklyn shipyards.

Brooklyn is a great commercial port. More than 70 steamship companies send their ships here from 200 foreign cities. Strange flags are common sights along the 25 miles of the Brooklyn water front. Recently new modern piers have been built, the Brooklyn-Port Authority Marine Terminal, that possesses the most advanced cargo handling equipment available. This includes container (boxes as large as freight cars) loading machines and huge 500-ton cranes capable of lifting a whole barge with its cargo. Over 3,000 people work at this terminal.

Brooklyn handles more freight than any other port on the east coast of the United States. Indeed, its warehouses have been called "America's biggest grocery store" because of all the foods stored within—tropical fruits, cloves, cheese, pepper, spices, sugar and coffee from the far reaches of the world.

In Brooklyn commerce and shipbuilding have gone hand in hand. In the past Brooklyn shipyards have turned out freighters, barges, and ferry boats. Then there is the Brooklyn Navy Yard, established in 1801, which has a long career of building warships: gunboats, frigates, battleships and aircraft carriers. In 1862, the first ironclad fighting ship, the *Monitor*, of *Monitor* and *Merrimac* fame, was launched here. The ill-fated *Maine*, blown up in Havana Harbor,

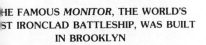

THE FAMOUS *MONITOR*, THE WORLD'S FIRST IRONCLAD BATTLESHIP, WAS BUILT IN BROOKLYN

was built here. During World War II, monster battleships of 45,000 tons were built in the Brooklyn Navy Yard. Among them was the *U.S.S. Missouri* upon which the Japanese surrendered. The 60,000 ton carriers *Independence* and *Saratoga* were also built here.

Although the Brooklyn Navy Yard does not build naval vessels any longer, in 1973 it launched the largest ship ever built in the United States, the 230,000 ton supertanker, the *Brooklyn* with the capacity of 9 million cubic feet of oil. Today, the Brooklyn Navy Yard has been turned into a center for many small factories producing articles such as mirrors, glass, furniture, and picture frames.

(Courtesy of the Port Authority of N.Y. and N.

AERIAL VIEW OF BROOKLYN PIERS

SHIPYARD AT GREENPORT

While building big ships seldom happens any more in Brooklyn, servicing already-built ships is still an important occupation on the water front. There are numerous repair facilities to service the big ships that stop at this port. The New York Dock Company and the Todd Shipyards Corporation are located in Brooklyn. The Todd drydock is one of the largest in the world capable of lifting the greatest ships.

For the rest of Long Island, boat building is mostly a matter of small craft. A lively business is carried on in the building of pleasure boats of all types, starting from rowboats to large yachts. At Greenport, fishing vessels and submarine chasers have been constructed as well as pleasure craft. As you drive along the coast roads, you can see these boats either on the ways in the small shipyards which lie outside of many villages on the island, or floating in the water in the countless harbors. On the North Shore we see many sailboats which can sail in the open waters of the Sound. Those on the South Shore are chiefly motorboats, some of which are capable of going out through the inlets into the ocean.

Servicing these pleasure craft provides employment for thousands of skilled shipwrights (carpenters), mechanics and other men. The boats must be built and repaired. They are caulked and painted every spring and stored away in the winter. This is done in shipyards, such as the ones located at Freeport Point, Glenwood Landing and Bay Shore.

Other industries are dependent upon these pleasure boats. Propellers are made by the Columbian Bronze Corporation at Freeport, the most important producer of small and medium sized propellers in the United States. There are also numerous yacht clubs on Long Island dependent upon business from the owners of pleasure boats.

THE AEROSPACE INDUSTRY

It is said that Long Island is the "cradle of aviation." It means that this is the place where aviation was protected and nurtured during its early childhood. Not only are there good airports, and not only did some historic flights take off from here but also the American airplane industry grew up on the Hempstead Plains.

The inventor-flyer who had the most to do with this was Glenn Curtiss. In 1918, during World War I, he built a major plant in Garden City to manufacture warplanes. It included research laboratories and three wind tunnels to test the aircraft. From this plant he turned out racers and passenger planes as well as military planes. His biplane racers won many prizes during the 1920's.

Since those times Long Island has been one of the leading airplane manufacturing communities of the nation. During World War II, thousands of military planes for both the Air Force and the Navy were produced here. These planes, mostly land or carrier fighters, contributed in no small degree to the winning of the war. The Republic Aviation Corporation (now Fairchild Republic), just out-

(Courtesy of Grumman Aerospace Corporation

GRUMMAN PLANE — F-14

side of Farmingdale, was the largest wartime producer of fighter aircraft in the world. At the peak of its output, Republic had 24,000 employees on its payroll, and they turned out more than 15,000 of their famous fighter plane, the *Thunderbolt*.

The Grumman plants, at Bethpage and Calverton, have specialized in military aircraft and spacecraft. During World War II, Grumman hired as many as 25,000 workers and turned out 600 planes a month, many of them for naval aircraft carriers. Some famous Grumman planes were the *Hellcat*, a World War II fighter, the *Panther*, a carrier jet plane, and the *Albatross*, a rescue plane for those shipwrecked at sea. At present the company produces the F-14 *Tomcat*, a swift, highly maneuverable fighter.

LUNAR MODULE ON THE MOON
"That's one small step for man, one giant
leap for mankind."
Neil Armstron
First Man on the Moo

that manufacture navigational equipment for both airplanes and ships. The Fairchild Camera Company turns out photographic equipment used on airplanes.

A more peaceful product of the Grumman Corporation is their LEM. It sounds like the name of some kind of a creature but it means Lunar Excursion Module. This was one of the space vehicles used by American astronauts to land on the moon. When the astronauts returned part of the LEM was left behind so that, to this day, a small piece of Long Island sits there in the cold moon light to show that earthlings once briefly stopped by.

There are a number of other companies connected with the aerospace industry on Long Island. Some of them make electrical equipment to control airplanes. This equipment may be placed in the plane, itself, or in the traffic control tower at the airport. Sperry Gyroscope and Sperry Rand are two large corporations

FAIRCHILD'S LUNAR MAPPING CAMERA

(Courtesy of Fairchild Camera & Instrument Corp.)

Let us visit one of the big aviation plants and see what goes into the making of an airplane. You can be sure it will be an exciting trip. Sightseers are not normally allowed within the gates of the great sprawling airplane factories because military planes are made, and the work is secret. But let us pretend that we have been issued a special pass by one of the company officials.

As we drive up to the main gate, a policeman stops us and asks what our business is. We tell him, and he directs us to the visitors' building. Inside the visitors' building a receptionist greets us and politely inquires as to our wishes. When we tell her that a company official has secured permission for us to visit the plant, she calls him on the telephone to check the truth of our statements.

After securing his approval, she gives each one of us a visitor's card with our name written on it which must be pinned in plain sight on some part of our clothing. We are then directed to the Administration Building where our friend, the company official, awaits us. He tells us that we are about to begin a tour of the main divisions of the plant. We will see how plane parts are made, how planes are assembled and how they are tested before delivery.

We are led to an adjoining building and upon entering, its huge size astounds us. It appears to be one of the biggest buildings in the world, so high and so wide that we can hardly see the other end. And the beehive of activity going on! There must be 5,000 men and women working at a thousand different jobs, all on the same floor.

Our guide tells us that there are thousands of parts, not counting bolts and rivets, used to make a modern military plane. Before the plane had been put into production, millions of engineering man-hours were spent producing 10,000 drawings. Hundreds of other engineers developed a plan for making large numbers of the aircraft.

The company official then leads us to the Parts Department where we see flat sheets of aluminum alloys and stainless steel formed into the needed airplane part shapes. Tremendous hydraulic presses, capable of a million pounds pressure, shape some parts in a matter of seconds.

From there we go to the sub-assembly lines, where the different sections of the plane are made. In one place, wings are being assembled. Across the way, the forward section of the body, or fuselage, takes shape under the riveter's gun. The bullet-proof wing tanks, the wiring systems and other parts are all taking form along these lines.

Our friend now leads us to the final assembly line, the last stage in the making of an airplane. Here, the plane is assembled with its different parts into its true shape. As we walk along the final assembly line, we watch the plane grow, somewhat similar to the way a tree grows.

First, the powerful jet engine, supported on a carriage specially built for the purpose is swung into the fuselage. Landing gear sprouts next from underneath the fuselage and from the tip of the nose. Then the airplane is given a tail assembly. Now the rapid-firing cannon makes its appearance in the nose. Finally, the fully assembled craft is wheeled out of the plant through the gigantic doors, given fuel and is ready for inspection. Thus a plane is born!

Outside the building, our guide explains that nothing is left to chance. Every part of the plane will be checked and rechecked. It is first tried out on the ground in several ways. If it passes this routine, it is then turned over to a company test pilot for a flight test. Upon passing a rigid flight test, the plane is turned over to an Air Force pilot for his "Okay." Then, and only then, will the Government buy the plane.

As we approach the landing strip of the company's private airfield we see a number of Air Force officers climbing into some of the aircraft lined up neatly along the edge of the field. Soon the jets are roaring. We are warned not to get behind the tails, for the hot gases shooting out could burn a man to death.

The planes make a great rushing noise and we cannot be heard as they taxi past us to the take-off point. Now they are in position and ready. The signal is given and they move forward in military formation, quickly gathering speed. In seconds they are in the air, lost to sight, leaving a thin stream of smoke behind them. Our friend tells us that in ten minutes those planes will be over Washington, D.C.!

LONG ISLAND AND THE ATOM

On the site of old Camp Upton, a former military camp, on the eastern end of Long Island, the United States Government has financed the building of Brookhaven National Laboratory. This is a scientific organization which does research in atomic (nuclear) energy. We all know the terrible destruction done by the atomic bomb at Hiroshima and Nagasaki (cities in Japan) during World War II. But here on Long Island we are finding ways in which the atom can be used to help mankind.

The Brookhaven National Laboratory is operated by a group known as Associated Universities Incorporated; it is administered by nine northeastern universities on behalf of all universities in the area. The Department of Energy of the Federal Government provides the money while the universities provide the "know-how" for the research at Brookhaven.

Brookhaven National Laboratory is situated on a 6,000-acre tract of land, and includes many buildings, some of which were formerly part of Camp Upton. These buildings house the laboratories, machine shops and offices necessary to carry on a research program in this new field. Approximately 2900 scientists, engineers and other staff members work here.

BROOKHAVEN NATIONAL LABORATORY

HIGH BEAM REACTOR (BROOKHAVEN NATIONAL LABORATORY)

When one enters carefully guarded Brookhaven, it is like going into a strange new world. In contrast with the bustling traffic in the nearby villages, it is a world of quietness and orderliness. It is a world of deep thinking and careful planning. It is a world of facts, rather than opinions—a scientists world. Some of the streets on the grounds are named after famous scientists who pioneered in the field of atomic energy. Also, you are apt to hear new words spoken such as cosmotron, nuclear reactor, synchrotron, alpha rays, positrons and neutrinos.

One Brookhaven research "tool" is its nuclear reactor used for creating energy for the experiments. The laboratory also has atom-smashers—"guns" that use electricity to speed up tiny particles which "break" atoms. One of these guns, called ISABELLE, is now being built at Brookhaven. Upon its completion in 1985 it will be the most powerful research tool of its type, capable of breaking up very small particles in the atom.

These devices are being used to discover new facts about atoms and about the energy which is locked up inside them. The scientists hope that this knowledge will help chemists, doctors, farmers and manufacturers. For example, research is being done on the effects of atomic rays upon living tissues—plants, animals, and their cells. Specific research projects at Brookhaven have included studies on:

> pollution in the environment
> the behavior of bacteria
> bone disease
> blood disease
> the structure of metals
> the safety of nuclear reactors.

Scientists from all over the world have gathered at Brookhaven to learn more about the mystery of the atom, and much will be discovered that was never before dreamed of.

SOME PROBLEMS

Forecasters predict rather gloomily that Long Island industry will decrease in the future, not increase. They point out that in recent times manufacturers have been moving from Long Island to other parts of the country. For example, from 1961 to 1976 Nassau-Suffolk lost 32,370 manufacturing jobs. We can expect this to continue, they say, with the possible exception of Suffolk County which keeps growing.

One reason given for this decline in industry is that Long Island is too dependent on foreign oil to run its industries. Petroleum imported from the Arab countries is expensive and may be shut off by the Arabs. It is hoped that oil will soon be discovered nearby, off the coast of Long Island. Also, the Long Island Lighting Company is building a nuclear plant at Shoreham to supply electricity. However, many people have objected to this because they believe that accidents may occur that will endanger Long Island lives.

An additional complaint is that Long Island is a "dead-end street." That is, there is no outlet for shipping Long Island products to other parts of the country by freight train or truck except through the New York City bottleneck. This is why some businessmen want to see a bridge built across Long Island Sound at the eastern end.

Another problem is the defense industry. It goes up and down like a yo-yo depending upon whether or not Long Island companies land fat government contracts. Thousands of workers may be laid off overnight if a large company fails to snare one of these contracts. For instance, this item appeared in *Newsday* on January 22, 1979:

> The defense programs of Long Island's largest employer, the Grumman Corporation, have received a heavy blow from administration budget cutters. . . . Grumman's livelihood rests with five major aircraft programs, three of which are substantially altered in President Carter's budget.

> The President proposed ending production of the Navy A-6E all-weather attack plane, slowing production of the Navy F-14 Tomcat from 36 a year to 24, and slowing the modification of the Air Force EF-111A, an electronic radar jammer, from five planes to two.

> That represents a $243 million reduction in defense spending at Grumman . . . and threatens at least 2,000 defense related jobs at the firm's Bethpage and Calverton plants.

The answer for this up and down swing of government contracts is to diversify—to make different kinds of things that can be sold elsewhere. The Grumman Corporation has been developing new lines of products to stay in business when military contracts do not come through. These products have included passenger plane parts, private business planes, hydrofoil boats, aluminum boats, and truck bodies.

WHAT WORDS ARE MISSING?

According to the statistics given in this chapter the Long Island county with the most amount of manufacturing is (1). The most important industry in Nassau-Suffolk is (2). The Human Resources Center in Albertson is famous for training (3) people how to work. Two reasons why ship building was an important industry on Long Island in the early days are (4) and (5). The name of the famous Civil War vessel built in the Brooklyn Navy Yard was the (6). The name of the flyer-inventor who started the aircraft industry on Long Island is (7). The Grumman Corporation is most known for its manufacture of (8). In order to keep going Grumman depends mostly on (9). Grumman also has manufactured the LEM, which is (10). The name of one company that manufactures navigational equipment for airplanes is (11). The Brookhaven National Laboratory is devoted to (12) research.

CHAPTER THINKING

1. Why is manufacturing such an important activity on Long Island? Give all the reasons that come to your mind.

2. Some people think that Long Island industry should turn away from manufacturing military equipment. What do you think of this idea?

3. There is some controversy over whether or not eastern Long Island should encourage the establishment of more factories. What are the arguments on both sides?

4. Many people are against the spread of nuclear energy plants on the grounds that they are dangerous. Do you think these people would include Brookhaven National Laboratory in their efforts to abolish nuclear plants? Give the reasons for your answers.

ACTIVITIES

1. Make a booklet covering manufactured articles on Long Island.

2. Take a trip to one of the important factories or to Brookhaven National Laboratory and report what you see to your class.

3. Draw a bar graph showing the manufacturing statistics given in the introduction to this chapter.

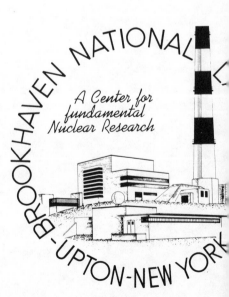

CHAPTER 9

Other Occupations on Long Island

There are many other occupations on Long Island besides those previously described in this book. This chapter concentrates on those found in Nassau and Suffolk counties. For example, some people make their living from buying and selling real estate. Also, there is the recreation industry. Retail businesses employ hundreds of thousands of workers on Long Island. These and other occupations make Nassau-Suffolk one of the wealthiest sections of the country. In 1978, the Nassau-Suffolk area ranked third in the nation as to the amount of money ($23,662) each household had to spend.

REAL ESTATE DEVELOPMENT

There is not a village of any size that does not have several real estate offices. Real estate refers to property, especially the buying and selling of land and buildings. Ever since 1639, when the Earl of Sterling sold Lion Gardiner a piece of land which is now considered part of Suffolk County, Long Island has been in the real estate business.

The reasons why Long Island has had real estate booms from the time it was first settled by white men are quite clear. From the beginning this land was considered rich farming country, and settlers were anxious to buy its fertile acres. Later, when New Yorkers began to look for places to live outside the crowded city, Long Island appeared as one of the most suitable places for them. It was just across the East River, and there were many pleasant places in which to build homes. Large estates were laid out by the more wealthy of these people. Vacationers, too, looked to Long Island as a good place to spend their holidays, so they bought land along the beaches and in the coves to build cottages in which to live during the summer. Around these demands the real estate business was founded and thrived.

Long Island communities seemed to spring up over night. In a period of ten short years what was once farmland became a little suburban village complete with small one-family houses, stores, gas stations, churches, schools, a theater, and a bank. This was the story of many Long Island communities, a story that repeated itself, again and again. It started in Brooklyn. The houses took over the old Dutch farmland in a complete victory. Next, the invasion of the homes spread to Queens, then followed by Nassau. There are a few farms left in these two counties but they are fast disappearing. The land became to valuable for a farmer to raise vegetables on it. Today, a small plot in an average community just large enough on which to build a house, if it could be found, will sell for $20,000. Farmers will not hold on to such valuable land to raise tomatoes.

At present Suffolk County is experiencing the same building boom that the three western counties went through during an earlier period. Although this county is still an important farming area the housing developments are taking large chunks out of the land.

Real estate depends upon many accompanying occupations. The houses may be built by small builders who build one, two or half a dozen houses at a time. Or, they may be mass produced by large companies that erect thousands of homes on large tracts of land that run into tens of millions of dollars of investment. For example, Levittown is a complete community of at least 18,000 homes built by one corporation.

To build these homes, stores and schools, there are the architects, the masons, the carpenters, the electricians, the plumbers, the landscapers, and countless other people who supply all kinds of building materials. Building is one of Long Island's chief occupations.

RECREATION AS AN ECONOMIC ACTIVITY

Long Island has been called "The Playground of New York." City dwellers take great pleasure in the relief from the noise and the heat of the big city which they find at the beaches and parks of Long Island. Providing for these vacationers has become a major industry.

Among our recreation occupations are golf, tennis, polo, auto racing, horse racing, baseball, football, fishing, duck hunting, picnicking, boating and swimming. In order to maintain these forms of recreation, it is necessary for thousands of people to service them—the part attendants, the caddies, the jockeys, the coaches, the lifeguards and, in some cases, the players themselves. Then, there are occupations which depend upon the recreation business. The fast food eating place, the motels, the gas station and the railroad derive much of their livelihood from the vacationers who travel to Long Island to enjoy a holiday.

Recently, a Long Island Tourism Commission has been established at MacArthur Airport to encourage people to spend their vacations on Long Island. It plans tourist activities such as tours of greenhouses and arboretums, husband-wife fishing weekends, and an amateur photography contest.

Long Island is a natural place for vacationing. Our fine beaches and ocean climate make a pleasant place to spend the summer. Our flat land is excellent for the construction of golf courses and tennis courts. Our indented shore line provides protected waters for small sailing craft. And, of course, our fishing grounds are always popular with the sportsman. Most important, Long Island is not far away for New Yorkers. They do not find it necessary to travel long distances before they reach their resort. Most of our recreation facilities are within fifty miles of Times Square. It is no wonder Long Island has become New York's playground.

Long Island was recognized as a resort area as early as 1664 when Governor Nicolls, the first English Governor, upon making an inspection trip, thought that the Hempstead Plains would be a fine place to have a race course. That same year the New Market Race Course was laid out and became a popular spot for Long Islanders and New Yorkers during the horse racing season. Soon other tracks at Jamaica, Huntington and Massapequa were built, and horse racing became a habit for the natives of Long Island. Today, there are three great Long Island horse racing tracks. Aqueduct and Belmont are located in Queens. Trotting races are held at the Roosevelt Raceway at Westbury in Nassau County.

ROOSEVELT RACEWAY

There are other spectator sports, too, those that a person watches instead of playing, himself. Here are some major league spectator sports played on Long Island.

Baseball: The New York Mets hit home runs at Shea Stadium in Queens.

Football: The New York Jets throw passes in Shea Stadium. They train at Hofstra University.

Hockey: The Islanders slam pucks at Nassau County Veterans Coliseum.

Tennis: World championship amateur matches are held once a year in Flushing Meadow Park in Queens.

Midget auto racing and stock car racing are popular at Freeport and Islip. Polo is played at the Meadowbrook Club in Westbury.

Long Island bathing beaches got a good start in the 1820's and 1830's when Rockaway became a fashionable "watering place," as it was called in those days—in other words, a place to bathe and swim, or sail and fish. The Rockaway and Jamaica Turnpike was built especially to provide an easy means of transportation for vacationers going to Rockaway. Since then the South Shore of Long Island has become a continuous bathing beach, 170 miles of the cleanest beaches in the world from Sea Gate in Brooklyn to Montauk Point. Jones Beach is one of the most beautiful ocean parks in our country. Fire Island and the Hamptons draw an international community of artists, authors and other celebrities to their surf. The excellence of Long Island's beaches attract some 70 million visitors each year, more than major league baseball, basketball and hockey combined. Other well known Long Island beaches include Coney Island, Manhattan Beach, and the Rockaways.

SAILBOAT RACING IS ONE OF THE FAVORITE SPORTS ON LONG ISLAND
Here we see an exciting moment in a race of the International Class Sailboats on Long Island Sound.

Golf was first introduced to America from its native land, Scotland. In 1891, a Scotsman by the name of Willie Dunn came to our country to show us how to play the game. He chose Shinnecock Hills, on eastern Long Island, to lay out one of the first American golf courses, because this place reminded him of his home in Scotland. Today, there are about 120 golf courses on Long Island. Many of them are private golf clubs and expensive to join. But some of them are public courses such as the Bethpage State Park golf course where people can play at a reasonable cost.

JONES BEACH

The state, the county and the town governments have done a magnificent job in developing parks on Long Island. These parks provide all sorts of enjoyment: picnicking, a place to play sports of every kind, nature walks, gardens, concerts, stage performances, and museums. The state parks on Long Island include the following:

Bayard Cutting Arboretum	Montauk Downs
Belmont Lake	Montauk Point
Bethpage	Nissequogue
Captree	Orient Beach
Caumsett	Planting Fields Arboretum
Connetquot River	Robert Moses
Heckscher	Sunken Meadow
Hempstead Lake	Valley Stream
Hither Hills	Walt Whitman House
Jones Beach	Wildwood

Two large county parks on Long Island are Eisenhower Park in Nassau and Weld Estate in Suffolk. Long Islanders can spend every weekend of the year in a different state, county, or town park without repetition.

JONES BEACH MAIN ENTRANCE
WATER TOWER AND PARKING FIELD

THE RETAIL BUSINESS

Earlier in this chapter we noted that Nassau-Suffolk residents ranked third in the nation in the amount of money they had to spend. In 1978 the people of Nassau-Suffolk all together had an income of $25 billion to spend. That's a lot of money! Much of this wealth is spent on the retail business—that is, people buy goods such as food, clothing, automobiles, radios and toys in the local shops and department stores to use for themselves. Since Long Island is mostly a region of homeowners we can expect a large amount of retail business. In a recent year retail sales in Nassau-Suffolk was over $9 billion, which made this region eleventh in the nation.

About 300,000 Long Islanders earn their living in the retail business. They work in candy stores and supermarkets, gift shops and department stores, and on main streets and in the bustling shopping centers.

Starting in the 1950's much of this shopping has shifted from the main streets of the villages to huge shopping plazas such as those found at Roosevelt Field in Garden City and Smith Haven Mall in Lake Grove. These are large, well planned shopping communities with several department stores, numerous small shops, restaurants, banks and other facilities all enclosed and protected from the weather. These pleasant places are well designed with wide malls and decorated with plants. The buyer can choose from many shops with a background of never-ending soft music played throughout the center. "Dentist's music," some people call it!

The Roosevelt Field Shopping Center, first established in 1957, is the second largest in the United States. The following statistics show this:

    Number of stores and services 179
    Weekly number of shoppers 300,000
    Annual sales $170,000,000
    Parking facilities . . . . 10,000 cars

This shopping center has its own guards to protect both the stores and the shoppers. It holds art shows and boat exhibitions in its malls. A Health Fair is held each year during which people can get a free heart test. And once a year Roosevelt Field conducts a Long Island Pageant to select a girl to send to the Miss Teenager of America contest.

A brief mention must be made about other service occupations on Long Island. These are jobs in which somebody performs a personal service for some one. For example, the auto mechanic repairs a car. Long Island provides hundreds of services from which people make a living. They include the services of school teachers, doctors, dentists, bankers, policemen, firemen, mailmen and many more.

SOME PROBLEMS

The growth of huge shopping plazas that usually are located on the outskirts of the villages has meant a decrease in business in the downtown section of some Long Island communities. Small stores located along the main street have been forced to close their doors because of lack of customers. The streets are almost deserted and empty stores are boarded up.

In an attempt to draw the buyers back some villages such as Hempstead and Freeport have tried urban renewal projects. That is, the main shopping street has been rebuilt to look attractive and provide a walking mall for shoppers. The stores have been redecorated. Nevertheless, thus far these urban renewal projects have not been successful in drawing a large number of customers.

Inflation is a serious problem for both businessmen and customers on Long Island. Inflation means that the price of a pair of socks that you bought last year for a dollar, this year costs $1.10. Every year there is inflation which runs about eight percent at present. In other words the income that a Long Islander makes is worth eight percent less each year. Unless he gets a raise in salary he will become poorer each year as inflation eats into his income.

Inflation hits retail businessmen. Store owners are forced to charge higher prices as their costs go up. Then people complain about the price of a steak, or a dress or a TV set and may not buy so many things.

Inflation hits other service occupations as well: doctors' bills go up, the auto mechanic charges more, and school taxes increase.

It has hit real estate. Everything costs more than it did previously; the cost of land, the price of lumber and other materials to build houses, and the wages of carpenters and other construction workers. Thus new houses cost more and many people cannot afford to buy them. That is one reason why the house building industry in Nassau-Suffolk has slowed down. During the 1960's an average of 17,500 new houses were built each year. During the 1970's this was down to an average of 11,500 homes.

GENERAL SUMMARY

In conclusion, it can be seen that Long Island is a highly important part of the United States. The amount and variety of its economic activities rate it near the top when compared to other areas. Its wealth surpasses that of many states. There are few places in the world which can offer its citizens such a wide selection of occupations in which they can earn a living. Its occupations are not limited to a few fields but cover a thousand types of work, some practiced on a large scale and some practiced on a small scale. This makes Long Island an interesting place to live and work.

WHAT WORDS ARE MISSING?

The occupation having to do with the buying and selling of land or buildings is called (1). The name of a famous large community on Long Island built by one corporation is (2). Two examples of occupations that accompany building are (3) and (4). Complete these names found on Long Island:

> two famous horse race tracks (5) (6)
> two well known beaches (7) (8)
> two state parks (9) (10)
> a famous polo field (11)
> a professional baseball team (12)
> a professional football team (13)
> a professional hockey team (14)

The largest shopping plaza on Long Island is (15). The name of the type of business in which customers buy products from stores to use themselves is (16).

CHAPTER THINKING

1. Why is real estate development one of the most important occupations on Long Island?

ACTIVITIES

1. Draw a map showing the state parks located on Long Island.

2. Make a picture booklet illustrating the different recreational facilities found on Long Island.

3. Pretend that you are a member of the Long Island Association, a super chamber of commerce for Long Island. Give a floor talk to a number of visiting businessmen pointing out why Long Island would be an excellent place for them to establish their business. Use all the chapters dealing with economic life as source material.

CHAPTER 10

Local Governments

The dictionary says that government is the control of human affairs. Whenever human beings are ruled by others or set up a rule over themselves we call this "government." As soon as a person is born, he begins to be governed, first by his parents, then in school, and later, as an adult, by society through its official units of government.

Just picture our community with no government whatsoever—no police to protect us, no fire department, no government-built roads, no traffic lights, and no rules to live by at all. While we sometimes resent the interference of government in our lives, we would soon discover that life without government is most uncomfortable.

There have been two main types of government in the history of humankind. There is the kind of government in which one man, or a small group of men, makes and enforces the rules for everybody. The whole community must abide by these laws or suffer punishment. This type of government is the kind which most people have had in the past, and it still exists in much of the world today. It has been known by several names, though the main practices are the same. The dictatorship and the absolute monarchy (a king's government) are in this class.

The other type of government is called democracy. Under democratic rule the people of a community set up their own government and decide through their representatives what the laws are to be. They elect a leader and other officers to see that the laws are carried out. But the leader depends upon the people for his power, and he stays in office only as long as he can get a majority of the people to vote for him. In general, this is the type of government found throughout cities and towns of the United States.

In a nation as large as the United States, stretching thousands of miles across the country and numbering 220,000,000 in population, it would be impossible for one government to make all the laws for all the people for every problem that arose in every community. Therefore, government in America is divided into several levels.

The highest level in our country is the federal government, the capital of which is located in Washington, D.C. This government looks after the country as a whole. Next, each state has its own state government which performs services for its citizens that the federal government does not supervise. Then there are the local units of government which make laws and carry out regulations allowed to them by the federal and state governments. They include the county government, the town government, the city government and the village government. All these levels of government are assigned special tasks, but they have one thing in common: they are all democratic.

In this chapter we shall devote our attention to that government which is closest to the people, the local government. Long Islanders seldom come into direct contact with the federal or state ruling bodies, but they often deal directly with the county, town, city and village governments into which Long Island is divided. When we wish to solve local problems, such as erecting a new traffic light in front of the school or having a new street cut through, we do not write a letter to the President of the United States nor do we send a committee to the Governor in Albany—those officials are much too busy looking after more important affairs. We notify the town, village or city government of our desires because these are the units which provide such local services.

It would not be practical to study the organization of every town, village, city and county governmental unit on Long Island, since there are far too many. Instead, the general practices of each of these types of government in Nassau and Suffolk counties will be presented with the understanding that there will be some differences among the various communities.

EARLY TOWN GOVERNMENT

In the beginning, government on Long Island meant town government. Thus we hear of the Town of Hempstead being settled in 1643 and the Town of Huntington being organized in 1653. The meaning of the word *town* used to be quite different from its present popular usage. Normally, when your mother says, "John, I am going downtown," or, "Sue, I'm going to town to the movies tonight," she is not using the word *town* as we shall use it in our study of town government. She means she is going to the shopping area of the most thickly populated part of your community. We shall use the word *town* to mean a subdivision of a county, including many unincorporated villages and rural areas, for the purposes of local government.

One of the first official acts of any group of colonists who settled on Long Island was to draw up a town government. Right from the start, lawlessness was carefully controlled and, as a result, we find that the history of Long Island towns was a peaceful and law abiding one.

The town government in the early days was in reality the town meeting. Once every spring, or whenever a special problem arose, the townsfolk were summoned to a meeting. Those who were freeholders, that is, men who were 21 years or over, who owned property in the town and who professed the particular religion of that town, were permitted to attend the meetings and vote.

When they met, they discussed the problems of the day, made regulations and elected officials who acted as authorities when the town meeting was not in session. Nothing was too small or unimportant for consideration at the town meeting. The townsfolk passed regulations dealing with every aspect of daily living, and many of the punishments for breaking these regulations were quite severe. The freeholders had the sole authority to grant or lease land, to select new ministers, to adjust boundary disputes and to grant mill rights. Their regulations covered such activities as pasturing cows, building fences and imposing fines for drunkenness or swearing.

They were quite worried about the morals of the community, as seen in some of their regulations. One town law read as follows: "Whereas, it has been too comen in this town for young men and maids to be out of their father's and mother's houses at unseasonable times of the night: It is therefore ordered that whosoever of the younger sort shall be out of his father's or mother's house past nine of the clock at night shall be summoned into the next court, and there to pay court charges, with what punishment the court shall see cause to lay upon them, except they can give sufficient reason for their being out late." Another town law frowned upon racing: "To whosoever shall run races, or run otherwise on horseback in the streets or within the town plot shall forfeit ten shillings to the use of the town."

The town meeting helped early Americans become democratic. People, meeting year after year to discuss and act on their own problems, soon got the habit of self government—a habit which in 1776, they refused to yield to the British king. In these early town meetings we developed our democratic ways. When we set forth as an independent nation, it was as a republic and not as a monarchy.

Today, because of the great increase in population, it is no longer possible to govern the town through a meeting of all its voters. In place of the town meeting, we now have a Town Board representing the people of the town, of which we shall hear more later.

As the towns grew in population and wealthh, it often happened that the people of a certain section wished to have their own local government, independent of town authority. So they petitioned the Town Supervisor to hold an election in that community to decide whether to incorporate the section as a separate village.

If the voters were in favor of such a proposition, the village was incorporated. This meant that they could set up their own government to make their own local laws. If a community was very large, it could request incorporation as a city and thus receive a larger measure of self government and local government powers.

By the 1970's there were 84 incorporated villages in Nassau-Suffolk raning in size from less than a hundred people to Valley Stream with a population of 40,000 citizens, the largest incorporated village in the United States. Outside of New York City there are two incorporated cities on Long Island—Glen Cove (26,000) and Long Beach (33,000) on opposite sides of Nassau County.

THE TOWN BOARD

At present there are thirteen towns on Long Island, outside of New York City, three in Nassau County and ten in Suffolk. Some of these towns have very

TOWN HALL AT HEMPSTEAD
The administrative offices of the Town Government are in this building.

large populations. For example, if the Town of Hempstead with a population of over 800,000, were a city it would be the ninth largest city in the United States. The towns are as follows:

   In Nassau County: Towns of Hempstead, North Hempstead and Oyster Bay.

   In Suffolk: Towns of Babylon, Brookhaven, East Hampton, Huntington, Islip, Riverhead, Shelter Island, Smithtown, Southampton and Southold.

The people of the town are governed by a Town Board which meets once a week in the Town Hall. The Board may be composed of from three to seven members, consisting of a Supervisor and from two to six Councilmen. In what are called *second class towns*, Justices of the Peace may be seated on the

THE TOWN BOARD MAKES THE LAWS FOR THE TOWN
Seated around the table, the Members of the Town Board discuss the problems of the town and decide what action should be taken.

Town Board instead of Councilmen. The Councilmen are elected by the voters of the town for four-year terms, but their election is so arranged that only half of them are elected every two years. This is to prevent a complete change of the membership of the Town Board at any one election. The Supervisor is elected for a two-year term. Town elections take place during odd-numbered years in order to avoid becoming mixed up with national and state elections during the even-numbered years.

The chairman of the Town Board is the Supervisor. The Supervisor takes charge of board meetings and votes with other members on any question which may come before the Town Board. While he cannot veto* ordinances (laws), he is considered the chief official of the town, and so he has many

* A veto is the refusal of an official to give his approval to a suggested law, thus preventing it from becoming law.

duties in carrying on the business of the town government. He compiles the town budget and determines how much money the town will need to meet its expenses and from what sources the money will come. Also, in Nassau County, he represents the town when the County Board of Supervisors meets in Mineola. We will learn more of this later.

The Councilmen, or the Justices of the Peace, meet with the Supervisor each week and together they adopt the regulations which will govern the people of the town. Private citizens may have the opportunity to voice their opinions and wishes on matters taken up by the Town Board by appearing at a hearing. Before the Board considers an important new proposal, the people are notified a few days before the meeting through the town newspapers. They then have the chance to prepare arguments for or against the proposal. At the hearing, citizens present their arguments, to which the members of the Town Board listen. Then the officers discuss it among themselves and take a vote. The proposal is either passed or rejected by a majority vote.

Town laws are passed regulating a variety of matters. Chief among them are the following:

1. Once a year the Town Board adopts a budget, fixing salaries for all employees of the town and laying out money for improvements throughout the town.

2. The town grants permits for many activities, franchises (permits) for bus lines, permits to build houses, to erect signs, to store gasoline, to run boarding houses, to build factories and for many othe purposes.

3. Roads, street lights, traffic signs and drainage come under the rule of the Town Board.

4. The Town Board has the power to appoint certain officials to run the various departments of the town government.

Assisting the Town Board in managing the affairs of the town, are several departmental heads and special boards, some elected by the people and others appointed by the Town Board. The number of departmental heads and special boards varies from town to town according to its size and class. In the following account of their work, it must be realized that not all towns have these officials. In the smaller towns one official may do the work which requires the efforts of several officials in the larger towns.

THE TOWN CLERK

The Town Clerk is the secretary of the town. He must keep all the writen records correctly. Among his duties are the following:

1. He must attend all Town Board meetings and record them in the permanent record, or the "ordinance book."

2. The Town Clerk must also keep other records of town business, including the old records dating from hundreds of years ago.

3. He may issue licenses and permits of various kinds, such as for marriages, for dogs, and for fishing.

RECEIVER OF TAXES

Anyone who owns land or a house soon becomes familiar with the Receiver of Taxes. Once a year this officer sends out various kinds of tax bills to property owners of the town. In addition to collecting taxes for the town, he collects taxes for the county, for the school districts and for other special government districts not considered directly part of the administration of town government. These include special districts such as, garbage collection, street lighting, water supply and fire protection districts.

THE ASSESSORS

If you become a home owner, one of the first things you will want to know is at what amount the Town Board of Assessors values your property. This board is charged with estimating the worth of every piece of property in the town. The purpose in doing this is for collecting property taxes. Property taxes are used to run the local governments. The more a piece of property is worth the more will be the taxes on it.

For example, let us say the value of a house is assessed at $10,000. This value is set upon it for tax collection purposes; it probably is worth a great deal more on the market. Then, let us say, the various local governments place a 30 percent property tax on this property. This means that the property owner must pay a 30 percent tax on each dollar of assessment, or a $3000 tax per year for a house assessed at $10,000. That's a high tax but not an unusual one on Long Island today.

If you feel that the Board of Assessors has valued your property at too high a figure, you may appear before it on a day set aside called "Grievance Day," and state your case.

Nassau County towns do not have a Town Board of Assessors because the County Government under its special charter has taken over this work for all three Nassau towns.

THE TOWN COMPTROLLER

Your town may have a Comptroller. The Town Comptroller is the person who has charge of checking on all sums and claims for the spending of town money. After the Town Board has authorized the spending of money, the

EACH NEW HOUSE THAT IS BUILT IS ASSESSED
The Town Board of Assessors estimates the value of the property. Then the property owner must pay a yearly tax on this amount to help run the local government

Town Comptroller sees to it that every town officer and department spends it only as directed. He issues warrants (permits to withdraw money) upon the Supervisor who acts as town treasurer.

SUPERINTENDENT OF HIGHWAYS

The Superintendent of Highways, as the title indicates, must take care of the town roads. He must repair them when they wear out, suggest new roads to the Town Board, remove the snow from the roads during the winter and make sure that there is proper road drainage.

THE TOWN ENGINEER

The Town Engineer has charge of all new construction in the town. He makes plans for the building of new roads, bridges and waterways, and makes recommendations to the Town Board concerning these. After a new road has been contracted for, he supervises the building of it.

THE TOWN ATTORNEY

The Town Attorney is a lawyer who is appointed to help the Town Board decide whether or not any action it desires to take will be according to the laws of the state. No Town Board may adopt an ordinance which is against state law, and it is the Town Attorney who advises on these matters. The Town Attorney also defends the Town Board in court in case the town should be sued by a private individual. He may also bring suit against anyone who does not comply with town regulations.

THE BUILDING DEPARTMENT

The Building Department is headed by the Town Building Inspector. This department issues permits for all buildings to be constructed within town limits. Before a person may secure a building permit, he must submit the plans for the house to the Building Department.

If these plans meet the building code requirements as adopted by the Town Board and if they do not conflict with zoning regulations, a permit is issued. While the building is in the process of construction, the Building Department sends out inspectors to see that it is being built correctly. A plumbing inspector examines all the plumbing so that no defective pipes are put into the house. Someone inspects the foundations and someone else inspects the electrical work. This is to insure that a safe building is being constructed, and one that will be a credit to the community.

The Building Department also makes sure that no building is erected in the wrong zone. The zoning ordinace divides the town into different types of building zones. There may be a "Residence A" district for the best type of one family houses; a "Residence B" for smaller houses; and "Residence C" for two family houses, hotels and boarding houses; a "Business" district for all the kinds of buildings found in a shopping center—stores, garages, and banks; and an "Industrial" district for factories. By putting these different kinds of buildings in different zones, our communities will become pleasanter places in which to live and do our work.

BOARD OF ZONING APPEALS

The Board of Zoning Appeals is composed of a group of people who listen to cases having to do with the zoning ordinance. If someone wishes to erect a building in a zone where that type of building is not permitted, he may appeal to this board. The members of the Board of Zoning Appeals will listen to the reasons why the zoning ordinance rules should be set aside. If it can be proven that there are good reasons for making an exception, the Board will permit it.

REGISTRAR OF VITAL STATISTICS

Some towns have a Registrar of Vital Statistics. The chief duty of this official is to keep a record of everyone in the town who is born and everyone who dies. Where there is no Registrar, the Town Clerk handles these matters.

THE JUSTICE OF THE PEACE

In addition to the Town Board and the town departments, the Town Justice of the Peace helps maintain law and order in the community. As we have already said, in towns where there are Justices of Peace, they may sit on the Town Board in place of, or with, Town Councilmen. However, they have other duties as well. They are the judges of the town and preside over certain types of court cases. The Justice of Peace may try small criminal cases, the more serious ones being turned over to the County Court. He may also try civil suits (a court case in which one person sues another) providing the case involves only small sums of money.

There are no Justices of the Peace in Nassau County towns because the local courts are divided into four District Courts which are part of the County Court system.

DEPARTMENT OF PARKS AND RECREATION

Town governments have a department to supervise the town parks. These parks provide all sorts of enjoyment: a swimming pool, an ice skating rink, a town beach, recreation programs for the handicapped, baseball fields, basketball courts and so on. Long Island is well provided for through these and other parks.

There are other town departments about which you can find information by writing to the Supervisor's office of the town in which you live. They include names such as:

Housing Authority
Industrial Development
Conservation and Waterways
Water
Urban Renewal
Safety
Traffic Control
Animal Shelter and Control

THE SPECIAL DISTRICT

Each town is divided into special districts for various purposes. For instance, a town may be divided into ten, fifteen or even twenty school districts, depend-

CHRISTOPHER MORLEY PARK

ng upon its size. Each district is given a number, such as School District Number One of the Town of Huntington.

There are special districts for the purpose of collecting garbage, providing street lighting, supplying water and maintaining a fire department for a certain area. Each of the older districts has its own independent commission or board elected by the people of the district to supervise these services. Each commission or board is a little government in itself doing the job for which it was created. However, some of these districts created after 1934 do not have their own government. They are administered by the Town Board.

THE SCHOOL DISTRICT

There are two general types of school districts on Long Island: the supervisory school district and the Union Free School District. The supervisory school district exists for smaller communities such as small villages and rural areas whose people do not wish to set up a special school district for their own small communities. The supervisory school district provides educational services for them and it covers a large territory.

However, for large villages, those with a population of 5000 or more, there is the Union Free School District. This is formed when the people of one or more villages join together to establish their own schools and, hopefully, get better education services.

The people of each school district have some voice in running the schools. One way in which they may participate in school affairs is to vote on the first Tuesday in May. On that day, every year, a school election is held. If a person is a qualified voter and (1) owns or rents property in the school district or (2) has a child who attends school in the school district, he is permitted to vote. He may vote for members of the Board of Education who are elected to serve for three-year terms. The Board of Education consists of from three to nine members and is responsible for supervising the local school system. People may also vote to approve or reject the school budget. The school budget includes such items as upkeep of the schools, construction of new buildings, the laying out of new playgrounds, etc. When a person votes during school elections, this is one way in which he or she expresses his approval or disapproval of what the schools are doing.

Of course, citizens and the School Board do not have the time to go into all the details in running a school system. Therefore, a Superintendent of Schools is hired by the School Board to do this. The Superintendent of Schools is an expert educator whose job it is to put into practice the wishes of the people of the school district. He must also obey State laws concerning education. He recommends to the School Board the hiring of teachers, the salaries of all school employees, and the buying of equipment. The School Board votes on whether or not it will accept the Superintendent's proposals.

VILLAGE GOVERNMENT

For the most part, the government of the incorporated village has the same power and provides the same services as the town does. Some of the officials are given different titles, but they have the same duties.

The chief officer of a village is the Mayor, who runs things. A Board of Trustees and the Mayor decide upon the village laws. There is also a Village Clerk. The larger villages may also have an Engineer, a Superintendent of Public Works, Street Commissioner, Treasurer and all the other officials as described for the town government. The judicial officer of the incorporated village is the Police Judge who has similar jurisdiction to that of the Justice of Peace.

CITY GOVERNMENT

The cities are not subject to town authority in any way. Indeed, New York City is the second most important ruling body in our state.

The City of Glen Cove has a Mayor who runs the government and a City Council that makes the laws. They are elected by the people.

However, the City of Long Beach has an unusual type of government; it has the "city manager plan of government." This city has an elected Council which makes the laws for the city. It also has a Supervisor who represents the city when the County Board of Supervisors meets. The person who runs things, however, is the City Manager, not elected by the people, but hired by the City Council. The City Manager is not a politician. He is appointed to administer city affairs regardless of party.

As with town and village government, the cities have a number of officials and departments that perform certain tasks. These have been fully described already for town government.

SOME PROBLEMS

One of the big problems in connection with local government is cost. Generally speaking, the local village, town and county governments and the special districts of Long Island serve the people well. However, they are expensive. They depend mostly upon property taxes to pay their bills. At present, when compared with 75 other similar metropolitan areas of the country, the Nassau-Suffolk area has the highest property tax of all. This high property tax is bad for several reasons:

1. Businessmen may not open new businesses on Long Island because of the tax.

2. Young people cannot afford to buy a house because of taxes.

3. Older, retired people find it difficult to hang on to their life-long homes because of rising taxes.

4. It is hard to sell a house on Long Island because of taxes.

Some people want to abolish the property tax entirely. They say that a property tax is a "regressive" tax because it hurts people with less money more than it hurts people with more money and that is unfair. Instead, they would like to have an income tax based upon salary and not on property. In this kind of a tax people who earn more would pay more. It is called a "progressive" type of tax.

Another local government problem is that there are so many of them. For example, Nassau County has three towns, two cities, 55 incorporated villages and hundreds of special districts for providing education, water, garbage removal, and fire protection. In 1979 a Nassau County official said there were 398 governmental units! Some critics argue, why don't we combine these small governments into larger units? It will be less costly and more efficient. We can eliminate a lot of jobs; for instance, we can have one superintendent of schools and his staff to run a larger school district instead of many superintendents and staffs for many small districts. Others argue back, "But we want to control affairs in our community."

SUMMARY

While we may be annoyed by the restrictions put upon us by government, we cannot do without it. Therefore, a democratic government is more acceptable to us because the people can control it, thus preventing it from becoming harsh and unreasonable. Town government is closest to the people. Through the old town meetings Americans have learned the meaning of democracy. Today, the town, village and city units of government perform many services in the community related to daily living for which the state and federal governments have no time.

WHAT WORDS ARE MISSING?

The main types of government in the world are (1) and (2). The three main units of local government treated in this chapter are (3), (4) and (5).

The earliest unit of government established on Long Island was the (6). The definition of a "town" as used in this chapter is (7). The name of the town in which you live is (8). The Town Board consists of a (9) and from two to six (10). The regulations of the town are passed by the (11). Private citizens may object to a proposed regulation during a (12).

Give one duty for each of the followiing officials:

(13) Town Clerk
(14) Receiver of Taxes
(15) Assessors
(16) Comptroller
(17) Superintendent of
     Highways

(18) Engineer
(19) Attorney
(20) Building Inspector
(21) Members of Board of Zoning
     Appeals
(22) Registrar of Vital Statistics

(23) Justice of Peace

The chief official of a village is the (24). Village ordinances are passed by the (25). Three types of special districts are (26, 27, and 28). Two cities found in Nassau County are (29) and (30).

CHAPTER THINKING

1. The old town meeting was the cradle of American democracy. Explain what this means and tell why this is so.

2. What are the ways in which you personally come into contact with the town, village or city government?

ACTIVITIES

1. Take a trip to your local unit of government and tell your experiences to the class.

2. Draw a chart showing the various parts of your local government and show their relation to each other.

3. There is considerable argument over whether or not a village should become incorporated or remain under the jurisdiction of the town government. Do some research on this and have a debate on the subject in relation to your own community.

4. Draw a map showing the counties, cities and thirteen towns on Long Island.

5. Keep a booklet of newspaper clippings describing the activities of local governments.

6. Invite a local government official to your class to speak about his work.

CHAPTER 11

The County Government

Except for the inhabitants who live in a few large cities, such as New York and Buffalo, the most important unit of local government for the people of New York State is the county government.

The county provides us with many things. First, it supplies us with those local services not already supplied by the town or village governments. Thus, it may maintain a police force, register important papers, build county highways, sewers and lighting systems, provide for the poor and offer free medical attention. These services are organized on a county-wide scale because it would be too expensive for each town and village to maintain its own separate departments. The larger county unit permits larger departments, with more financial support, and therefore with better equipment.

Next, the county acts as an agent of the state. Many state laws are left to the county for enforcement, including the prosecution of criminals, the maintenance of traffic regulations and the supervision of health conditions. The county collects taxes through the Town Receiver of Taxes for the state. It issues state automobile licenses and drivers' permits. Thus, the government in Albany depends upon each county to reach the local community to put its rules and regulations into effect.

THE HISTORY OF COUNTY GOVERNMENT ON LONG ISLAND

As we noted in the previous chapterm, the first kind of government established on Long Island was the town government, covering a certain limited area. In the early days, this was quite satisfactory because each Long Island town was almost a little world in itself, cut off from the rest of the island by the wilderness. But by the time the English took control of New York in 1664, the number of towns and the population of the colony had increased to such an extent that larger divisions of governmental authority were needed.

Therefore, in 1665, the English Governor, Nicolls, summoned the respresentatives of the Long Island towns to Hempstead in order to introduce a new code of laws. They were known as the Duke's Laws, after the Duke of York. Under the Duke's Laws, Long Island, along with Staten Island and part of Westchester, was to be known as Yorkshire. In England a shire was equivalent to a county. Furthermore, Yorkshire was to be divided into three ridings, a riding being a subdivision of a shire. The towns in Suffolk County formed the East Riding; Kings County was included in the West Riding; and the rest of the Island was in the North Riding.

The shire type of government lasted only a few years. The people were quite discontented with the Duke's Laws because they failed to provide for an assembly to which they could send their own representatives. Government was strictly in the hands of the Governor. In 1683, the Duke of York, after many petitions, consented to the establishment of an assembly and also abolished the three ridings. New York was organized into ten counties, among which were the Long Island counties of Kings, Queens and Suffolk.

For more than two hundred years, the county organization on Long Island remained unchanged. Then on January 1, 1899, a new county, Nassau, was formed. This came about as a result of the incorporation of Greater New York City in 1898, composed of the boroughs of Manhattan, The Bronx, Staten Island, Brooklyn and Queens. The section of Queens County, which lay outside of New York City, became Nassau County.

The names of the Long Island counties are interesting. Kings County was named after King Charles the Second of England, ruling monarch during the time the county was established. Queens was named in honor of his wife, Catharine of Braganza. Suffolk gets its name from Suffolk, England, the birthplace of the first settlers of that region. Nassau is so called after the old name of Long Island. Shortly after the English took control from the Dutch, many of the Dutch names were changed to English. Long Island became Nassau Island in honor of the reigning English monarch, William of Nassau. This name was never too popular in its time. In 1899, when the new county was formed, the people decided to call it Nassau County, in memory of the old name of Long Island.

PRESENT DAY COUNTY GOVERNMENT

The center of county government, or the county seat as it is called, is located for Nassau County at Mineola and for Suffolk County at Riverhead. In both places you will find beautiful new buildings in which are housed the various county offices. The Nassau Court House is one of the finest buildings in the county. This is flanked by other, smaller, new county buildings. There is also the Old County Court House, now headquarters of the County Executive and the Board of Supervisors. In Suffolk, a building program in the late 1950's resulted in another beautiful county administrative building group.

Nassau and Suffolk counties have the "county executive plan of government." This plan gives to the county much of the power and many of the jobs ordinarily held by towns and villages. This centralized scheme of government has resulted in the saving of much money and has helped develop more efficient service to the local communities.

We shall now discuss four parts of the county government:

1. The County Executive.
2. The county departments.
3. The county legislative body.
4. The county courts.

AERIAL VIEW OF NASSAU COUNTY'S BEAUTIFUL NEW COURT HOUSE

QUEENS COUNTY COURTHOUSE IN JAMAICA

THE EXECUTIVE OF THE COUNTY

An executive is a person who is given the job of managing a particular activity. There are business executives for running factories, department stores and wholesale houses; there are executives who run clubs such as the Elks or the Lions; and there are executives for running governments.

Nassau and Suffolk have County Executives to run their governments. In Nassau the County Executive is elected for three years, while in Suffolk he is elected for four years. It is their responsibility to administer the government properly and according to the laws.

The most important single job that the County Executive has is the preparation of the budget for each year. Since it costs much money to provide the many county services, the County Executive must estimate how much money will be needed for all governmental departments. He must also determine from what sources this money will come.

The County Executive has the power to appoint certain officials of the county government. Many departmental heads are chosen by him. He does this by recommending to the county legislative body (explained later) that certain people be appointed to certain jobs. If the legislative body confirms the appointment the person will get the position. If the legislative body rejects the recommendation the County Executive must make a new recommendation.

The County Executive also participates in the work of the county legislative (law-making) body. The Nassau County Executive presides over this body when it meets. The County Executive is not permitted to vote but, should a tie occur, the County Executive may cast the deciding ballot, thus breaking the deadlock. Also, this official has the power to veto any measure which he does not approve. If this should happen, the bill becomes a law only when two-thirds of the legislative body vote in favor of it. Otherwise the bill will not become a law.

Running a county government is a tremendous undertaking. Therefore the executive branch of county government has been divided into many departments with each one specializing in a particular field. The head of each of these departments is normally given full responsibility in conducting its business. The work of some of these departments is presented in the following paragraphs.

THE COUNTY CLERK

Veterans who returned from the Armed Forces were urged by their commanding officers to have their discharge papers registered when they got home. Many of them did this so that if their original discharges were lost, they could always refer to these registered papers.

PETER F. COHALAN,
SUFFOLK COUNTY EXECUTIVE, 1981

The place where papers are registered is the County Clerk's office. This office has on file thousands upon thousands of all kinds of official papers, or copies of them. There are records of property deeds, mortgages on houses, land maps and countless others. Many of these records are preserved through microfilming, a process by which a picture is taken of the original paper and reduced to the size of a postage stamp. In this way, a great number of documents can be filed in a small space. The County Clerk's office also issues drivers' licenses and automobile license plates.

THE COUNTY COMPTROLLER

The County Comptroller is the person who safeguards the money of the county. Before any money can be spent, it must have the Comptroller's approval. He must also know from what sources the money is to come. He investigates all account books, all contracts and all purchase orders for each of the county departments. He also may look into money matters of any town or special district in the county.

THE COUNTY TREASURER

The County Treasurer has charge of handling all the money of the county. He collects the money, deposits it, and then pays it out when requested by the proper authorities. You may get him confused with the Comptroller. Remember, the Comptroller authorizes the claims for payment of money according to the law, but the County Treasurer, after being authorized by the Comptroller, does the actual handling of the money.

Each month the Tax Receiver in each town and city of the county must send the County Treasurer any taxes which he has received for payment of state or county taxes. The Receiver of Taxes also notifies the County Treasurer when taxes are not paid. The County Treasurer then tries to collect these taxes. If the person who is behind in the payment of his taxes refuses to pay within a reasonable period of time, the County Treasurer institutes law proceedings to force that person to pay or else be deprived of his property.

THE DISTRICT ATTORNEY

Probably the most exciting official of all is the District Attorney, or "D.A." as he is commonly called. Television has so greatly popularized his work that he seems like an old friend. The District Attorney is expected to prosecute people who commit criminal acts. Robbery, blackmail, assault, kidnapping and murder are criminal acts. Contrary to what you see on television shows, the District Attorney seldom captures a criminal personally. This is left to his bureau of investigation or to the police force. After the criminal is jailed, he is brought before the county court. The District Attorney, or one of his assistants attempts to prove the guilt of the person suspected of crime. In addition to prosecuting the guilty, the District Attorney must be careful to protect the innocent from being charged with crimes they did not commit.

DENNIS DILLON, NASSAU COUNTY
DISTRICT ATTORNEY, 1981

THE COUNTY MEDICAL EXAMINER

The County Medical Examiner is a doctor employed by the county to investigate any suspicious-looking deaths. If murder or suicide is suspected, the County Medical Examiner makes a complete examination to discover the cause of death.

THE POLICE DEPARTMENT

The most important law-enforcement agency in the county is the County Police Department. The police arrest criminals, investigate disturbances, direct traffic and, in general, maintain the peace. At its headquarters building in each county you will find a radio station, teletype machines, a detection laboratory, a complete file of all persons arrested in the county and even a Laundry Mark Bureau by which persons may be traced through the laundry marks on clothing.

The county police system maintains precincts throughout the county. Each precinct has its own captain and police force. The county police look after all the unincorporated areas in the towns of the county. However, any incorporated village which maintains its own police force can elect to join the county police if it so desires.

THE NASSAU COUNTY POLICE ARE IN CONSTANT TOUCH WITH OTHER LAW-ENFORCING AGENCIES BY TELETYPE AND OTHER MEANS OF COMMUNICATION

THE SHERIFF

The Sheriff helps maintain law and order in the county. He has charge of the county jail. He acts as warden and looks after the prisoners. He is responsible for summoning people to court who are involved in civil law suits, that is court actions which have nothing to do with crime. He also notifies people who have been ordered to serve on juries.

THE COUNTY ATTORNEY

The County Attorney has a position similar to that of the Town Attorney. He advises the county government of the legality of its acts. When he is requested by the county legislative body, he words the ordinances which they pass in legal language so that there is no misunderstanding as to what they mean. He defends the county when it is being sued. Sometimes he goes to Albany to try to get legislation which the county desires passed by the state.

THE PLANNING COMMISSION

In the past, too often Long Island communities grew helter-skelter without any plans. They became eye-sores. Beautiful land areas were gobbled up by business and homes. Population became crowded. Waterways became polluted. Roadways became choked with automobile traffic. Factories came and went with their jobs. This is why the County Planning Commission was established.

The job of the Planning Commission is to recommend to the County Government what steps to take to make our communities good places in which to work and live. It recommends a great variety of changes such as:

> zoning regulations to separate industrial areas from
> residential areas,
> the building of parks and recreation facilities,
> the development of transportation facilities,
> the provision of health service,
> the development of commerce and industry,
> the use of waterways,
> and many others.

PUBLIC WORKS DEPARTMENT

One of the largest departments in the county is the Public Works Department, headed by a Commissioner of Public Works. The department has charge of all county activities which are of a building and maintenance nature. Its most important jobs are the construction of new roads and the repair of old ones. The Department of Public Works also supervises the building of bridges, sewers, drains, incinerators and public buildings. It is responsible for the removal of snow from the highways. It makes traffic surveys and recommends the placement of stop lights and other traffic signals. It also has charge of the water system.

DEPARTMENT OF RECREATION AND PARKS

To a large extent Long Island is a residential community—a place where people live. This is why parks and recreation facilities are so needed. People want to get outdoors and enjoy themselves and Long Island has just about every kind of recreation imaginable. Much of this is provided by the county government in parks ranging in size from tiny, vest-pocket neighborhood triangles to large areas such as Eisenhower Park in East Meadow. There is something for everyone, from the toddler to the senior citizen. You can ice skate in August and browse in a museum in December. There is music for the rock fan and for the symphony lover. You can play golf, tennis, softball, football, basketball, shuffleboard, badminton, corquet and bocci! Nassau County has 5,000 acres of parklands and wildlife preserves, while Suffolk has 18,000 acres.

THE HEALTH DEPARTMENT

The activities of the Health Department are varied. First, this department keeps a record of the status of health throughout the county and keeps the public informed. Next, this department supervises all communicable diseases, that is, diseases which can be spread from one person to another very easily. Diseases such as smallpox and measles are quickly isolated when discovered.

The Health Department also maintains a family care division where parents are taught how to care for babies or what to do if someone is sick.

The sanitation division of the Health Department supervises all food and water for the county. Drinking water, swimming places and sewage disposal are checked monthly. Garbage collection and incinerator plants are supervised by this department. All milk must meet its approval and a check is made upon bakeries, restaurants, and butcher shops in an effort to prevent disease carried by food. In Nassau County the Health Department works in cooperation with the Nassau County Medical Center, a county owned hospital.

SOCIAL SERVICES

This department helps take care of the needy in the county. Poor people may receive aid from the Department of Social Services when they cannot find work. Homes are found for children who have no homes and they are turned over to foster parents instead of being placed in an orphan asylum. Those who need medical care, but cannot afford it, are given free dental and medical service. This department maintains the county home for old people who have no place to go. It also extends aid to the physically and mentally handicapped.

NASSAU COUNTY MEDICAL CENTER IN EAST MEADOW

THE BOARD OF ELECTIONS

A Board of Elections is charged with conducting election proceedings at voting time. It is headed by two commissioners, one a Republican and the other a Democrat, who are appointed by the county legislative body on the recommendation of the County Chairman of each political party. It is the duty of this Board to see that the proper election machinery is placed throughout the county for the voters' convenience. They see to it that the balloting is done honestly and that the counting of votes is done accurately.

THE CIVIL SERVICE COMMISSION

The Civil Service Commission is a body of people who supervise the hiring of county employees. If one wishes to work for the county government, he must make application through the Civil Service Commission. His qualifications are examined and he may be given a competitive test. Those who make the highest scores on the test may be hired first. The Commission also supervises working conditions and the salaries for governmental employees. All county employees, except departmental heads, are under the Civil Service Commission.

THE NASSAU COUNTY LEGISLATIVE BRANCH

The legislative branch of any government is the branch that makes the laws. In the case of Nassau County, it is called the Board of Supervisors. This Board is composed of six supervisors elected from Nassau's three towns and two cities. (The Town of Hempstead elects two Supervisors because of its large size.) The Board is presided over by the County Executive.

The voting strength of each representative varies. The County Executive has no vote except in case of a tie. The Supervisors have a weighted vote depending upon the size of the town or city from which the Supervisor comes. Supervisors from more populous places have more votes than those from smaller places. Thus we find the vote weighted as follows:

Town of Hempstead Supervisor	31 votes
Town of Hempstead Supervisor	31 votes
Town of Oyster Bay Supervisor	28 votes
Town of North Hempstead Supervisor	21 votes
City of Glen Cove Supervisor	2 votes
City of Long Beach Supervisor	2 votes

These weighted votes show that if the Supervisors from the Town of Hempstead vote together (62 votes) they will win over the rest of the County (53 votes).

The Board of Supervisors meets once a week. At that time it considers business affecting the welfare of the county. The Board decides ahead of time what it will take up at a certain meeting. The calendar, as it is called, must then be posted, that is, notices must be put up on the bulletin boards and printed in the two official newspapers for the county, one a Republican paper and the other Democratic. These notices inform the public of what will be considered at the next meeting. Then, interested citizens can be present to give their opinions on the subject.

The Board passes upon many types of legislation. The budget must be adopted. It passes legislation on many activities, including construction work, borrowing money, and creating new departments of government. The Board also approves the County Executive's appointments to office.

THE SUFFOLK COUNTY LEGISLATIVE BRANCH

The Suffolk County legislative body is different from that of Nassau County. First of all, it is called the Suffolk County Legislature, not the Board of Supervisors. Also, its members are called Legislators, not Supervisors, and they are elected every two years only for the purpose of serving in the County Legislature; they do not head town or city governments at the same time. Furthermore, each Legislator has only one vote; he or she does not have a weighted vote as in Nassau. The Legislators elect their own Presiding Officer. Lastly, there are eighteen members of the Legislature who represent smaller districts with approximately equal populations in comparison to the unequal and larger districts of Nassau.

THE JUDICIAL BRANCH OF COUNTY GOVERNMENT

The executive branch enforces the laws which the legislative branch makes. In carrying out the law, the members of the executive branch, notably the District Attorney, may bring before the County Judge someone accused of breaking the law. The judge must determine, or a jury must determine, whether or not the accused person is guilty of breaking the law. Then, the judge must decide how much punishment should be given to the guilty person. This all comes under the head of interpreting the law. Interpreting the law may also involve civil suits, as well as criminal actions, in which one person may sue another whom he considers has wronged him.

There are a number of different kinds of county courts. First, there are the District Courts found throughout the county. Each District Court Judge is elected for six years. This court tries cases which are not very important. Civil suits up to the amount of $6000 may be brought to the District Court. Criminal cases considered in this court are mostly minor ones such as a driver of an automobile passing a red light or a man disturbing the peace. Minor criminal cases are called *misdemeanors*, while the more serious ones are called *felonies*.

The County Court tries the more important cases. It is presided over by a County Court Judge elected for a 10 year term. This court may try civil suits up to the amount of $10,000. In very serious crimes such as murder, it may, under certain conditions, invoke the death penalty as punishment.

The County Court works in cooperation with a Grand Jury. This jury is a panel of men and women who are outstanding citizens of the county, selected from lists prepared by the Commissioner of Jurors.

The District Attorney turns over to the Grand Jury the names of persons suspected of crime and the evidence to bring the suspect to trial. If there is enough evidence the Grand Jury will then charge the suspect with having committed a crime and he will have to stand trial; that is, he is indicted.

The case is then tried in court before a Trial Jury, composed of twelve men and women acceptable to the court and to the opposing attorneys in the case. The District Attorney, or one of his assistants, then attempts to prove to the jury that the defendant (person accused of the crime) is guilty. At the end of the trial, the jury goes into another room to decide the guilt of the defendant. If he is declared guilty, the judge may give the maximum penalty, or he may give a lesser penalty depending upon what he thinks of the case.

The Family Court hears cases involving families and children. Children under the age of sixteen are brought before this court when they have committed a serious offense. Court procedure here is not so strict and the judge will try to help children who have made their first mistake. Also this court tries cases involving youths between the ages of 17 and 20. Parents who do not take proper care of their children or who are cruel to each other may be brought before this court to try to change their behavior.

The Surrogate's Court is an entirely different type of court. The Surrogate Judge, elected for six years, has to do with the settlement of wills and estates. All wills must be taken to the County Surrogate and be identified by him. He sees to it that the terms of the will are carried out. Sometimes he appoints a guardian for a child who is left with no one to look after his interests.

SOME PROBLEMS

In Nassau many people criticize the form of County Government. They say that it is unfair because the six-member Board of Supervisors does not truly represent the one and a half million people who live in the county. First of all, because of their weighted votes, the two Supervisors from the Town of Hempstead can rule the whole county. They have 62 out of 115 votes. If they want, they can outvote the rest of the Board again and again.

Secondly, the critics say, the two major political parties, the Republican and the Democratic parties, are not fairly represented. For example, in 1978, the number of registered voters enrolled in each of the two parties was as follows:

Party	Number of Registered Voters	Percent of Total of Registered Voters
Republican	316,980	48
Democrat	233,144	35
Others	110,594	17

However, during the election of that year the Board of Supervisors became solidly controlled by one party, almost as if the other party did not exist:

Position	Party	Weighted Vote
Town of Hempstead Supervisor	Republican	31
Town of Hempstead Supervisor	Republican	31
Town of Oyster Bay Supervisor	Republican	28
Town of North Hempstead Supervisor	Republican	21
City of Glen Cove Supervisor	Democrat	2
City of Long Beach Supervisor	Democrat	2

In other words, the Republican Party controlled 97 percent of the votes on the Board of Supervisors while the Democrats had a voting strength of only 3 percent. Yet 35 percent of the registered voters in the County were Democrats. "It's robbery!" scream the Democrats. They believe that a County Legislature as found in Suffolk County would be much fairer. It would break up the extreme voting power possessed by a few Supervisors and distribute it more equally to a larger number of Legislators.

GENERAL SUMMARY

This is the story of local government on Long Island, the government closest to the people. We live in a democracy; our local officials are elected by the people. If we hope to have good laws made and wise men to administer them, then we must be careful in electing our officials. A good citizen tries to elect intelligent office holders. We must follow the actions of the present government and weigh them against the claims of the opposing parties. We try to keep ourselves informed about public problems. We, ourselves, participate in government when called upon. A good citizen respects the rule of the majority. When a law is made he obeys it and if it happens to be an unfair or undemocratic law he works to have it changed.

WHAT WORDS ARE MISSING?

In 1665, the (1) laws were announced to delegates assembled in Hempstead. Kings, Queens and Suffolk counties were formed in the year (2). Nassau County was formed in the year (3). The county you live in is named in honor of (4). Your county seat is located at (5).

The head of the Nassau and Suffolk county governments is called the (6). A person who is in charge of things is called an (7). The legislative branch of government (8) the laws. In Nassau the county legislative body is known as the (9). In Suffolk it is called the (10).

The judicial branch of government (11) the laws. Important court cases are tried in the (12). The (13) is the body which decides whether or not a person is to be brought to trial. Wills are settled in the (14) court.

Give one power or duty for each of the following officials.

(15) County Executive
(16) County Comptroller
(17) County Clerk
(18) Sheriff
(19) District Attorney
(20) Commissioner of Public Works
(21) County Treasurer

(22) County Attorney
(23) Commissioner of Police
(24) County Medical Examiner
(25) Commissioner of Health
(26) Civil Service Commissioners
(27) Commissioner of Social Services
(28) Commissioners of Elections

CHAPTER THINKING

1. The opening paragraph of this chapter claimed that the most important unit of local government is the county government. What evidence is there to support this claim?

2. Suppose a person is accused by the D.A. of robbing a bank. What steps must be taken before he can be sent to prison?

3. Which do you think is better, the Nassau County Government or the Suffolk County Government? Why?

ACTIVITIES

1. Keep a booklet of newspaper clippings describing the work of your county government.

2. Take a trip to your county seat and describe your experiences to your class.

3. Attend a court case and report on it to your class.

4. Invite a county official to your class to talk about his work.

CHAPTER 12

Persons and Places

By now you must be well aware of Long Island's high place in the history and present day life of the nation. From the time of Hudson's voyage westward across the great ocean to Long Island shores to the day of Lindbergh's trail-blazing flight eastward from Long Island to Paris, our story has been the story of America.

This chapter will introduce you to cultural life on Long Island. By culture we mean the artists, the poets, the writers and musicians; the paintings, the poetry, the books and the operas; the museums, the libraries, the colleges and the orchestras; we mean anything a people possesses which aids in the improvement of the mind. One way in which we judge the superiority of nations of the past is through their cultural works. Thus, we place ancient Greece near the top in the history of great peoples while the Hottentots of Africa are scarcely noticed.

Long Island is endowed with some of the finest cultural institutions of the country. In this chapter we will visit some of the old houses and listen to some of the old tales. We will meet some of the outstanding men and women who have made Long Island history. We will also get a glimpse of our education institutions—the colleges, the libraries, and the museums that bring learning and enjoyment to our millions.

COLLEGES AND UNIVERSITIES

Long Island has a large number of institutions of higher learning. These are colleges and universities where young people gain advanced knowledge and prepare for professional and business careers. By county they include the following:

Brooklyn: Brooklyn College
Polytechnic Institute-New York University, an engineering school
Pratt Institute, specializing in architecture and commercial art
Long Island University
St. John's University
St. Francis' College
St. Joseph's College
Brooklyn Law School
State University of New York Medical Center
Cathedral College
Kingsborough Community College
New York City Community College

HOFSTRA UNIVERSITY

Queens: Queens College
St. John's (Long Island Division)
Queensborough Community College
York College
La Guardia Community College

Nassau: Adelphi University
Hofstra University
C.W. Post College
Molloy College
New York Institute of Technology
Webb Institute of Naval Architecture
State University at Westbury
Nassau County Community College which is run by the
county government
The United States Merchant Marine Academy, a school built
by the Federal Government for the purpose of training

officers for the merchant marine. The discipline and routine at this Academy are very much like that at West Point. There are parades, inspections, guard duty and many other practices found in a military establishment.

Suffolk: State University at Farmingdale
State University at Stonybrook, one of the best of our state universities specializing in mathematics and science.
Dowling College
Friends World College, a Quaker institution devoted to promoting world peace and a global outlook on life.
Polytechnic Institute, for engineering.
Southampton College
Suffolk County Community College, supported by the County

LIBRARIES

The largest library on Long Island is the Brooklyn Public Library. In addition to the main building, just off Prospect Park, it has dozens of branch libraries scattered throughout the Borough of Brooklyn, serving the inhabitants in their home communities. The Queensborough Library system is second in size with its main building located in Jamaica.

Among our historical libraries is the scholarly Long Island Historical Society, in Brooklyn, which houses many of the old papers and books dealing with the Long Island of the past. In Suffolk County, the East Hampton Library is also noted for its historical works. The precious Morton Pennypacker collection there consists of a group of books and papers devoted to the history of Long Island. Throughout the rest of Long Island, each community is served by its own small library, an independent organization set up by the local inhabitants for their enjoyment and education.

MUSEUMS AND GARDENS

Long Island has many interesting museums and beautiful gardens open to the public. Many of them are free-of-charge or charge only a small entrance fee so that everyone can enjoy them. Here are some of them by county.

Brooklyn:

The Brooklyn Museum is one of the most modern museums in the country. Within its walls you will find exhibits dealing with hundreds of different subjects. It contains some of the finest paintings in the world. The displays of metal work, pottery making, basket weaving and oriental ceramics are fascinating to see. It has an excellent African collection and also a complete collection of colonial costumes. Long Islanders will be especially interested in the full scale reproduction of an old Dutch house.

The Botanical Gardens located in Brooklyn contain rare specimens of plants from all over the world.

UNITED STATES MERCHANT MARINE ACADEMY AT KINGS POINT

The Brooklyn Children's Museum has a collection of exhibits appealing to young people. Here one can see exhibits of animals, birds, and minerals. Miniature models are arranged in a series to show the history of the United States and of other peoples. Boys and girls especially like this place because of its delightful activity program. There are picture puzzles to make, games to play, books to read and models to construct, all relating to the exhibits on display.

Nassau:

The Tackapausha Museum and Preserve at Seaford shows Long Island plant and animal life. It has five miles of nature walks and live animals.

The Old Bethpage Village Restoration is a rebuilt community showing life as it existed on Long Island before the Civil War. It has farms, barns, a country store, a school, church, and houses as they existed in the 1840's. The attendants wear costumes of the time and some give demonstrations of skills practiced in those days. A visit to this place is like stepping back 150 years in time.

The Black History Museum in Hempstead shows the part blacks have played in both the past and present on Long Island.

The Museum in the Park, at Eisenhower Park, shows special exhibits from time to time.

Garvies Point Museum and Preserve specializes in Long Island archeology and geology. One of its features is an Indian archeological excavation.

(Courtesy of Nassau County Historical Museum

OLD BETHPAGE RESTORATION VILLAGE

Also, Hangar Number One of the former Mitchel Air Force Base is being rebuilt as Nassau County's first air and space museum. It will exhibit old airplalnes and present space vehicles.

At Oyster Bay there is Planting Fields Arboretum, a large park-like area with unusual plants from the tropics and other places, kept in hot-houses.

Suffolk:

One of the most interesting places in Suffolk County is called The Museums at Stonybrook. This is a collection of buildings and exhibits showing the past. It contains an excellent collection of carriages, an old time one-room school house, a grist mill for grinding grain, a blacksmith shop, and an art museum. The art museum has the best collection of paintings by the famous Long Island painter, William Sidney Mount.

The Suffolk County Historical Museum, in Riverhead, holds displays from early Long Island including the John Hulbert flag which some people say is the first American flag, made even before the famous flag of Betsy Ross. This flag has thirteen red and white stripes, and thirteen stars on a blue field, but the stars are arranged in a diamond shape instead of in a circle.

The Hecksher Museum is found in Huntington. The Parrish Art Museum is located in Southampton, and Sag Harbor is reminded of its former chief occupation by a Whaling Museum.

The Bayard Cutting Arboretum near East Islip has some fine nature walks displaying beautiful plants.

(Courtesy of Nassau County Historical Museum)

SAG HARBOR WHALING MUSEUM

SOME OLD PLACES

Long Island is about as old a settled place as one can find in our country. The first whites came here in the 1630's, only fifteen or twenty years after the initial settlement at Plymouth. There are still standing several old buildings and churches dating from the 17th and 18th centuries. A visit to some of them would help us understand the life of those times.

Brooklyn:

In Brooklyn there are old Dutch houses. One of the finest examples of Dutch colonial architecture is the Lefferts House in Prospect Park, built in 1777 and furnished in the Dutch style. The Moody House is in Gravesend. Lady Deborah Moody began the English settlement of Gravesend in 1643 while New York was still under the Dutch.

(Courtesy of Nassau County Historical Museum)

LEFFERTS HOUSE

Queens:

The King Mansion is located in Jamaica. Here lived Rufus King, member of the Convention which drew up our Constitution, Ambassador to Great Britain and United States Senator from New York State.

The Bowne House is found in Flushing. Built in 1680 by the Quaker, John Bowne, it soon became a popular meeting place for the Society of Friends. Bowne led a life of ups and downs. Because of his Quaker preachings, Peter Stuyvesant had him bound in chains and sent to Holland to stand trial. However, the Dutch authorities were more liberal than their Governor in New Netherlands, and Bowne was acquitted. He came back and plunged into his Quaker preachings more ardently than before. George Fox, the English founder of the Society, was entertained by him. William Penn, Quaker proprietor of the colony of Pennsylvania, also visited Bowne at his Flushing residence.

With the growth of this religious sect, Bowne's house became too small to hold the Quaker meetings. Therefore, in 1694, a Friends' Meeting House was erected in Flushing which still stands. During the Revolutionary War, British soldiers used this building as a barracks and a hospital.

(Courtesy of Nassau County Historical Museum)

BOWNE HOUSE, BUILT IN 1661

Nassau:

Nassau County has its Friends' meeting houses, too—one located at Matinecock dating from 1725 and the Jericho Meeting House near Westbury built in 1788. The visitor is impressed with the extreme severity of the architecture and the lack of color in these buildings. The Quakers believe that undue

OLD GRIST MILL RESTORED INTO RESTAUR.

adornment is sinful. Yet the meeting houses have a beauty of their own. While their lines are simple, they have an air of soliditiy and steadfastness, a sign of the Quaker faith.

On the subject of churches, Christ's First Presbyterian Church and St. George's Episcopal Church, both in Hempstead, claim a long and eventful career. The Presbyterian Church was established by Richard Denton in 1644 while St. George's was organized in 1693 and chartered by King George II of England in 1735. Though these are two of the oldest church organizations on Long Island, neither of them is housed in the original building. The present Presbyterian church building was erected in 1847 while the St. George building dates from 1822.

Roslyn has an old grist mill built in the early 1700's which now serves as a restaurant. An old paper mill also stood there, erected in 1744, the first paper mill in the State of New York. It is said that when George Washington toured Long Island in 1790, he stopped at the Roslyn paper mill and under the guidance of the owner, Henry Onderdoonk, made a sheet of paper for himself. The paper mill burned down some years ago but a replica standing on the site serves as an American Legion headquarters.

ROSLYN PAPER MILL

RAYNHAM HALL

Ini Manhasset Valley Park is, perhaps, the oldest one-room school on Long Island. Built of wood in 1826, it has been beautifully restored by the county.

Rock Hall in Lawrence and Raynham Hall at Oyster Bay are two old mansions with fascinating histories. First built in 1740 by Samuel Townsend, and since enlarged, Raynham Hall is full of colonial bric-a-brac. There are also two the the great links from the iron chain that stretched across the Hudson River at West Point during the Revolutionary War.

After the capture of Long Island during the Revolution, Raynham Hall became a British headquarters. Colonel Simcoe, of the Queens Rangers, was quartered there and so was a handsome young British officer by the name of Major John André. While the Townsend family objected to having their home taken over by the British officers, they could do little about it. There were three pretty girls in the family, Audrey, Sarah and Phoebe, who quickly became the attraction of the British officers. In a series of glass panes above one of the doors, you can still see where one of them scratched with a diamond the words "adorable Miss Sarah."

THE MANHASSET VALLEY SCHOOL IN MANHASSET VALLEY PARK
This is Nassau County's oldest one-room school. Dating back to 1826, it was built when less than 3,000 people lived in the town of North Hempstead.

Now Sarah's brother, Robert Townsend, was one of Washington's most trusted spies. He managed to get word to his sister that a British secret agent operated from somewhere in the vicinity of Raynham Hall, and he asked her to keep a sharp lookout. One day a man came to the house and slipped a letter into one of the kitchen cupboards, addressed to a Mr. James Anderson. Sarah, who had watched this unobserved, became curious. Upon the stranger's departure, she examined the letter. She knew no one by the name of James Anderson in the neighborhood, so she returned the letter to its hiding place and waited to see who would claim it.

Soon Major André came into the kitchen with the excuse of getting some doughnuts. While Sarah had her back turned, he hastily pocketed the letter and left. Sarah decided to watch André.

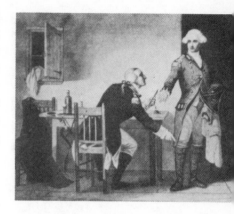

BENEDICT ARNOLD TELLS ANDRÉ TO HIDE PLANS OF WEST POINT IN HIS BOOT

Not many days later, she heard a hushed conversation between André and Simcoe concerning something about West Point. Quickly she sent a message to her brother. And so, later, when Major André was captured, the whole story came out how Colonel Simcoe, Major André and the American General, Benedict Arnold, plotted to betray West Point. André was hanged as a spy, Arnold escaped to the British, while Simcoe mourned the loss of his friend and the failure of his plans.

Josiah Martin of Antigua came to Lawrence, and in the year 1768 built Rock Hall. This beautiful mansion became one of the most notable residences of colonial times. There were parties, fox hunting and elaborate meals, with which Martin entertained distinguished visitors from Europe and the West Indies.

Martin was appointed Royal Colonial Governor of North Carolina in 1771. Because of his stern treatment of rebellious subjects, he became looked upon as a much hated Tory. When the Revolution broke out, he was forced to flee from New York to his North Carolina estate. But with the British occupation of Long Island, he returned to his Rock Hall home. At the end of the war, in spite of the persecutions of all Loyalists on Long Island, Martin stayed here and held on to Rock Hall.

Suffolk:
Sagtikos Manor, at West Islip, is another old Long Island mansion. This great manor house was originally built in 1697 with additions being erected at a later date. During the Revolution, the British general, Sir Henry Clinton, made his headquarters there for some time. George Washington slept at Sagtikos Manor during his Long Island tour in 1790. The bedrooms of each of these famous persons are furnished as they were at the time.

At Cutchogue stands what is claimed to be the oldest English house in New York State. Appropriately, it is called the "Old House" and dates from 1649. But the citizens of Oyster Bay dispute this claim and argue that the Job Wright House in their own village should receive the honor of being considered the oldest house on Long Island.

Among the old churches in Suffolk there are the Caroline Episcopal Church and the Presbyterian Church, both in Setauket. Caroline Church was built in 1729, and its square tower leans something like the leaning tower of Pisa. It was named in honor of Queen Caroline, wife of King George II, who presented the church with a communion service in 1730. The present building of the Presbyterian Church was erected in 1811, though the church was founded long before that time.

Clinton Academy, in East Hampton, is what we now consider the first high school in New York State. After its erection in 1784, the father of John Howard Payne taught there.

"Home Sweet Home" is located in East Hampton, too, where Payne spent his youth.

(Courtesy of Nassau County Historical Museum)

THE "OLD HOUSE" AT CUTCHOGUE

CREATORS OF GREAT WORKS

Long Island is not lacking in literary nor artistic geniuses. This has been the birthplace, or adopted home, of many a writer and painter. Among them the following people are outstanding.

Walt Whitman:

Of all the great creative artists who trod our Island lanes, the name of the poet, Walt Whitman, shines the brightest. Born at West Hills, Suffolk County, he was a Long Islander to the very marrow of his bones. From 1819 to 1892, his life span, he loved to roam the Long Island hills and skirt the Long Island shores, enjoying the wonderful sights that he found in nature.

While still a young man, Whitman went to Huntington and learned to be a printer. In a short while he started a newspaper, *The Long Islander.* Later, he became editor of the *Brooklyn Daily Eagle.* Then he left his Long Island hills to live in the busy city of Brooklyn. But Whitman never stayed in one place for long. At the age of thirty-five, he resigned his *Eagle* post so that he could devote more time partaking of the life of a rapidly expanding America. He explored the country and spoke with all kinds of people.

Whitman called himself "the poet of democracy," and he wrote his poems about the greatness of the common man. His most noted collection is *Leaves of Grass* in which he sings of the growth of America.

WALT WHITMAN

Whitman loved Long Island, and many of his poems contain references to the land of his birth. "Starting from Fish Shaped Paumanok" and "Songs of Long Island" are two of them. Perhaps you will like this opening stanza about his childhood in the poem "Out of the Cradle Endlessly Rocking."

> "Once Paumanok
> When the lilac-scent was in the air and Fifth-month grass
>   was growing,
> Up this seashore in some briers, two feather'd guests
>   from Alabama, two together,
> And their nest, and four light-green eggs spotted
>   with brown;
> And every day the he-bird to and fro near at hand,
> And every day the she-bird crouched on her nest, silent,
>   with bright eyes,
> And every day I, a curious boy, never too close, never
>   disturbing them
> Cautiously peering, absorbing translating."

William Cullen Bryant:

Another Long Island poet, this time by adoption rather than by birth, is William Cullen Bryant (1794-1878). Bryant came from Massachusetts where as a young man he gained world reknown for his poem, "Thanatopsis." This poem is written in an American style about the great facts concerning life and death. Because he broke away from European traditions in writing poetry, Bryant is called the "Father of American Poetry." On Long Island he took up residence in a house he called Cedarmere in the village of Roslyn. For fifty years he edited the *New York Evening Post* and wrote poems in his spare time.

"HOME SWEET HOME" AT EAST HAMPTON

John Howard Payne:
Here was a Long Islander who spent more of his time away from his homeland than in it. Perhaps this is what prompted him to write the beautiful song, "Home, Sweet Home."

Born in 1791 in New York City, his parents moved less than a year later to a little cottage at East Hampton. Thus, Payne spent his youth on the east end of Long Island. While still young, Payne began to write plays, several of them becoming New York hits. He then became a successful actor and from the New York stage he journeyed abroad where he continued to act and write plays. He spent twenty years in England and France and wrote sixty plays. In 1823, while in England, Payne wrote his famous "Home, Sweet Home" about his little cottage at East Hampton.

He returned to America in 1832 but, with his appointment as consul to Tunis by President Polk in 1842, he left again for foreign shores. Payne died in Tunis in 1851.

William Sidney Mount:
This artist was one of four brothers, all talented painters, born in Setauket. With the death of their father the Mounts went to live with their uncle, Micah Williams, at Stony Brook. William was the most gifted of the Mount brothers, and his paintings hang in such famous art galleries as the Metropolitan Museum of Art and the Brooklyn Museum.

WILLIAM SIDNEY MOUNT

If you lived near Stony Brook during the first half of the nineteenth century, you may have been astonished to see a queer looking contraption approaching down the road. Mount traveled the countryside in a horse-drawn wagon enclosed on one side with a large plate glass. Inside was his traveling studio and a stove to keep him warm during the winter as he journeyed from place to place painting Long Island scenes. Undoubtedly, this was the forerunner of our present day auto trailer!

William Sidney Mount is famous for his barnyard scenes. He loved to put on canvas the little things that happened around the farm. You will like the rural scenes painted in "Cider Making," "Raffling the Goose," "Turning the Grindstone," "Bargaining for a Horse," and "The Dance after the Sleigh Ride." His "The Banjo Player" is a life-like portrait of a Long Island Negro-Indian.

Other Creative Long Islanders:
America's first successful opera writer and first published Negro poet were Long Islanders. Micah Hawkins, uncle of the Mount brothers, wrote such operas as "The Sawmill" and "A Yankee Trick." Jupiter Hammon, who lived in Queens Village, published the first of several poems in 1760. They were of a religious nature.

Benjamin Thompson is known for his *History of Long Island*, a three volume work published in the 1830's. This was the first important Long Island history to be written. It is the source for much of our information about early Long Island.

Christopher Morley, a recent writer of international fame, lived in Roslyn. One of his most popular books is *Parnassus on Wheels*.

STATESMEN, POLITICIANS AND OTHER MAKERS OF HISTORY

Several Long Island leaders have taken a hand in shaping the history of America. During their time, their words and their deeds were well known throughout the land.

William Floyd, born in Brookhaven in 1734, has a long and distinguished record in the service of his country. He was an ardent patriot. He signed the Declaration of Independence in 1776. For this and other rebellious acts, his estate was appropriated by the British when they captured Long Island. Floyd acted as delegate to the Continental Congress from 1774 to 1782. He became a Major General in the New York State Militia and later represented Long Island in the House of Representatives of the first United States Congress. He died in 1821.

Another Revolutionary War figure was Ezra L'Hommedieu, a French Huguenot of Southold, who represented Suffolk County in the Continental Congress. He helped form the New York State Agricultural Society and wrote extensively about agriculture.

A great Quaker name on Long Island is that of Elias Hicks. Hicks lived and preached at Jericho—when he was home. Much of his time was spent traveling around the country spreading the teachings of the Society of Friends to thousands who came to hear him. In 1827, due to his more liberal interpretation of Quakerism, a split occured in Quaker ranks. The Orthodox Quakers remained strictly in accord with the teachings of George Fox while those who followed Hicks became known as "Hicksite Quakers." So at Old Westbury you will find two meeting houses side by side, that of the older Orthodox Quakers and the other the newer Hicksite Quaker building. Most Long Island Quakers today are Hicksites.

One of the most powerful speakers ever to live in Brooklyn was Henry Ward Beecher, minister of the Plymouth Congregational Church. Beecher was a relentless opponent of slavery. In the middle 1800's, Sunday after Sunday, he denounced this evil from the pulpit. He made many enemies but, not lacking in courage, he continued his attacks on slavery until the whole nation was aroused. His sister, Harriet Beecher Stowe, added fuel to the fire with the publication of her book, *Uncle Tom's Cabin*. The Beechers lived to see slavery abolished forever in the United States.

"TEDDY" ROOSEVELT & FAMILY, CIRCA 1904

"Teddy" Roosevelt, twenty-fifth President of the United States, took his family to live at Oyster Bay. He remembered the fun he used to have as a child when he visited his cousins there, "hunting, exploring and cheerfully risking their necks in and about the woods and waters of Long Island's north shore." So he built a home facing Long Island Sound and called it Sagamore Hill. Here he wrote and studied and organized bird clubs. When he became President, in 1901, Sagamore Hill became the Summer White House. It is now a fascinating museum complete with furnishings of the time.

The story of "TR's" activities would fill many pages. He wrote history books; was a great naturalist; fought in the Spanish American War at the head of the famed Rough Riders; hunted and explored in the far reaches of the world; became Governor of New York State; was elected Vice President of the United States, and, upon President McKinley's assassination in 1901, became President.

Other notables in Long Island's story include Admiral Alfred Thayer Mahan of Woodmere and later of Quogue. He was a famous naval historian who wrote a much quoted book entitled *Influence of Sea Power in History*. Henry L.

Stimson was another Long Island resident. He was United States Secretary of War from 1911 to 1913. He became Governor General of the Philippines in 1927, was Secretary of State during President Hoover's administration and, in 1940, was called upon by President Franklin D. Roosevelt to again become Secretary of War.

We have saved our pirate for last. Captain William Kidd is not a Long Islander—but his name is so linked with stories of buried treasure and mysterious midnight meetings on Long Island shores that we consider him our very own. Here is his story.

The wealthy merchants and the King's officers of the Royal Province of New York were greatly disturbed. Ship after ship which left the protected waters of New York Bay was pounced upon by bold pirates who waited off the coast, robbing and burning. Something had to be done, so it was decided to equip a fighting vessel to hunt down the outlaws of the ocean and bring them to justice. William Kidd was chosen to lead the expedition, since he was an upright and capable sea captain.

In 1695, Kidd and his crew sailed for Madagascar and the Red Sea, hangouts of the pirates. But during the trip, the crew mutinied, we are told by Kidd, and forced him to turn pirate. They led an adventuresome and profitable life, tracking down unsuspecting ships.

Captain Kidd, tiring of the uncertainties of piracy, decided to return to America and give himself up, hoping that the English Governor, the Earl of Bellomont, would protect him since Bellomont was one of the chief sponsors of the original venture. This is where Long Island enters the picture.

One evening in June of the year 1699, John Gardiner, third Lord of the Manor of the Isle of Wight (Gardiners Island) "noticed a mysterious six-gun sloop riding at anchor off the island, but gave no sign . . . Lord John waited patiently for two days and then on the second evening rowed out to visit the stranger sloop." He was ushered into the presence of Captain Kidd, himself. Kidd made some polite inquiries. He also asked Gardiner to take care of two Negro boys and a Negro girl for him. The next day he requested that six sheep and a barrel of cider be sent to him, and for their trouble the pirate give the Gardiners four pieces of gold. Then he sailed away.

Three days later back came Kidd. This time he landed with some chests, one of them a box of gold. He told Gardiner about his proposal to give himself up to the Earl of Bellomont, relying upon the Governor's mercy, and he ordered the Lord of the Manor to keep in trust for him the treasures he had brought ashore. The chests of gold were buried in the swamps with the warning that they just remain untouched if the members of the Gardiner family hoped to retain their respective heads.

The pirate sailed for Boston where the Earl of Bellomont was staying. In Boston Captain Kidd was quickly put in irons and sent to London for trial. Tried and condemned, he was hanged on Execution Dock May 12, 1701.

Long Islanders have looked for Captain Kidd's treasures for a long time, for it has been whispered that the pirates riches are still hidden in secret places along the island's shores. Perhaps some day you will find a gold sovereign in the sands, or a red ruby—or a blood stained dagger!

CAPTAIN WILLIAM KIDD BECAME A PIRATE

INDEX